SCHOLASTIC

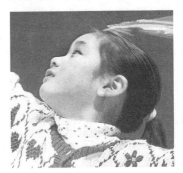

NONFICTION PASSAGES
With
Graphic
Organizers
for
Independent Practice

GRADES 2–4

by Alice Boynton and Wiley Blevins

NEW YORK • TORONTO • LONDON • AUCKLAND • SYDNEY
MEXICO CITY • NEW DELHI • HONG KONG • BUENOS AIRES

Teaching Resources

Text Credits: Joke from LITTLE GIANT BOOK OF SCHOOL JOKES edited by Charles Keller, published by Sterling Publishing Co. Copyright © 2000 by Charles Keller. Reprinted by permission. "Go, Animals!" "From Grapevine to Jelly Jar" "Creature Feature" "Bat at Night" "One Language, Many Nations" "Seeds on the Go" "8 Reasons to Love an Octopus" "Pilgrim Children" "How Spiders Use Silk" "Hot Spot" "Tooth Truth" "Penguins of the World" "Stamp of Excellence" "Zoos Help Out!" "Chinese New Year" "Horsing Around" "Making Crayons" "A Chief in the Family" "Care for Our Earth" "Blast-Off!" "Sew Many Secrets" "Our Presidential Past" "Critters Cry for Help" "Spinning for a Good Cause" "Celebrating 100 Years of the World Series" are reprinted from SCHOLASTIC NEWS. Copyright © 1996, 2000, 2001, 2002, 2003, 2004 by Scholastic Inc. Reprinted by permission. "Digging Bones" "Dinner Time!" "House With a Trunk" "Could Your Body Go to Mars?" are reprinted from SUPERSCIENCE. Copyright © 1998, 2001, 2003 by Scholastic Inc. Reprinted by permission. "Animal Survival" is reprinted from Life Science Essential Concepts Card 8. Copyright © by Scholastic Inc. Reprinted by permission.

Photo and Illustration Credits (Interior): Title page: (clockwise from top left): Theo Allofs; The Granger Collection, New York; Tui Di Roy/Minden Pictures; AP Wide World; Raymond Dobard, Silver Springs, MD; Werner H. Muller/Peter Arnold; Jimmy Dorantes/Latin Focus.com; Page 4: Illustration by Mike Moran; Page 9: (top) Chase Swift/Corbis, (bottom) Stephen J. Krasemann/DRK Photo; Page 10: (top) Stuart Westmoreland/Stone/Getty Images, (bottom) AP Photo/Morry Gash; Page 13: Michael Newman/Photo Edit; Page 14: (top left) Courtesy of Welch's, (center right) Courtesy of Welch's (center left) Grafton Smith, (bottom right) Michael Myers/Welch's, (bottom left) Grafton Smith; Page 16: Illustrations by Ellen Appleby; Page 17: Stephen Hird/Reuters/Landov; Page 18: (top) GK Hart/Vikki Hart/The Image Bank/Getty Images, (center) Cyril Laubscher/Dorling Kindersley/Getty Images, (bottom) Keith Alstrin/Index Stock; Page 21: (top) Theo Allofs, (center left) National Geographic/Getty Images, (center right) Animals Animals, (bottom left) M. Harvey/DRK Photo, (bottom right) Stanley Breeden/DRK Photo; Page 22: (top left) Theo Allofs, (top right) Frans Lanting, (center left) Theo Allofs/The Image Bank/Getty Images, (center right) University of Florida/IFAS/Tara Piaso/AP Photo; Page 25: (top right) Mapman/Scholastic, (center left) Jimmy Dorantes/Latin Focus.com, (center right and bottom) Laura Dwight/Photo Edit; Page 26: (top) Lawrence Migdale, (center) Jeff Greenberg/Photo Edit, (bottom) David Simons/Stock Boston; Page 29: (top left) Illustration by John Carrozza/Scholastic, (top right) Werner H. Muller/Peter Arnold, (bottom) David Cavagnaro/Peter Arnold; Page 30: (top left) Kevin Schafer/Peter Arnold, (top right) Fred Bruemmer/Peter Arnold, (center) Scott Camazine/Photo Researchers, (bottom) Lawrence Migdale/Stock Boston; Page 32: (left) David Cavagnaro/Peter Arnold, (center) Werner H. Muller/Peter Arnold, (right) Scott Camazine/Photo Researchers; Page 33: Illustration by John Carrozza/Scholastic; Page 34: Illustrations by Karen Beckhardt/Scholastic; Pages 37 and 38: Ted Curtin; Page 41: (top) Adam Jones/Photo Researchers, (bottom left) Robert & Linda Mitchell, (bottom right) Dr. Paula Zahl/Photo Researchers; Page 42: (top) Dwight Kuhn, (center) Robert & Linda Mitchell, (bottom) Courtesy of Pam Langer; Pages 41 and 42: Illustrations copyright (c) 1995, 1989 by Bruce Degen from THE MAGIC SCHOOL BUS series by Joanna Cole. Published by Scholastic Press/Scholastic Inc. Used by permission. The Magic School Bus is a registered trademark of Scholastic Inc.; Page 45: (top) Richard T. Nowitz/Corbis, (inset) Mapman/Scholastic; Page 46: Illustration by Ian Warpole; Page 49: (top) Dan Sudia/Photo Researchers, Inc, (bottom) Photodisc via SODA; Page 50: (top) Kenneth W. Fink/Photo Researchers, Inc, (bottom) Photodisc via SODA; Page 53: (top) Keith Srakocic/Associated Press, (bottom) AP Photo; Page 56: (top) Wayne Lynch/DRK Photo, (bottom) Johnny Johnson/DRK Photo; Page 57: (top) Digital Vision, (bottom) Fritz Prenzel/Animals Animals; Page 58: (top) Tui Di Roy/Minden Pictures, (bottom) Roger de la Harde/Animals Animals; Pages 56-58: Maps by Mapman/Scholastic; Page 61: (top) Courtesy USPS, (bottom) Ric Francis/AP Photo; Page 64: (top) Kevin Schafer/Corbis, (center) Jessie Cohen/National Zoological Park/Smithsonian Institution, (bottom) Robert J. Hoage Phd./National Zoological Park/Smithsonian Institution; Page 65: (top) Robert J. Hoage Phd./National Zoological Institution, (center) Jessie Cohen/National Zoological Park/Smithsonian Institution; Page 69: (top) A Ramey/PhotoEdit, (center) Don Smetzer/Getty images, (bottom) Ap Wide World; Page 72: Michael Geissinger/The Image Works; Page 76: (top) Photo courtesy of Binney & Smith/maker of Crayola Products, (bottom left and right) Gale Zucker/www.gzucker.com 2003; Page 77: Gale Zucker/www.gzucker.com 2003; Pages 80 and 81: Lisa Rudy Hoke/Black Star; Page 84: Discovery Pictures/BBC; Page 85: (left) Martin Dohrn/SPL/Photo Researchers, (right) John & Maria Kaprelian/Photo Researchers; Page 88: Lawrence Migdale; Page 89: (top) Harrison Northcut, (bottom) Tom Fant/Natural Light Images; Page 90: Courtesy Tree Musketeers®; Page 92: Illustration by Karen Stormer Brookes; Page 93: courtesy Millenium Jet, Inc. © 2000, 2001, 2002 Millennium Jet, Inc., Illustrations by Mike Moran; Page 96: Raymond Dobard, Silver Springs, MD; Page 97: The Granger Collection, New York; Page 100: 5W Infographic; Page 101: (top) C. Lockwood/Animals Animals, (bottom) Kevin & Sue Hanley/Animals Animals; Page 102: (top) Norbert Wu/Minden Pictures, (bottom) Norbert Wu/Minden Pictures; Pages 105 and 106: All photos courtesy of the Save Lucy Committee and used with permission. All rights reserved.; Pages 109 and 111: (left) Library of Congress via SODA, (right) National Archives via SODA; Page 112: (left) Kevin & Sue Hanley/Animals Animals, (right) Dorling Kindersley/Getty Images; Page 113: (left) B.G. Thomson/Photo Researchers, Inc., (right) Gary Meszaros/Bruce Coleman; Pages 116 and 117: Illustrations by Ron Barrett; Page 120: J. Barry Mittan, Illustrations by Mike Moran; Page 123: Bettmann/Corbis.

Photo Editors: Amla Sangvhi and Daniella Nilva

Photo Credits (Cover): Children: Dave Bartruff/Corbis; Octopus: Reuters/Corbis; Willie Mays: Hulton Archive/Getty Images; Crayons and Penguins: Photo Leader.

Every effort has been made to acquire permission to use the materials in this book.

Cover design by Brian LaRossa
Interior design by Melinda Belter

ISBN 0-439-59018-3

5 6 7 8 9 10   40   12 11 10

Contents

Introduction

Is there any one of us who hasn't experienced the challenge of teaching nonfiction? A lesson on the circulatory system can cause heartburn; a lesson on tornadoes can leave your head spinning! But we ourselves have always loved reading nonfiction, so we're always searching for engaging ways to turn our students on to the wonders of the world. What we've discovered is that many of our students share our enthusiasm for this genre. This has encouraged us to include more nonfiction in our reading curriculum. That's why we created *Nonfiction Passages With Graphic Organizers for Independent Practice Grades 2–4*. The nonfiction passages in this book:

- provide easily-graded, purposeful homework practice correlated to your content area curriculum.

- help you communicate to parents their child's growing reading skills and content area knowledge.

- support both your reading and content area curriculum.

- provide an inexpensive and instant way to increase the amount of nonfiction students read each week.

- are a natural extension of students' reading, science, and social studies class work, not just busy work for homework.

We hope you and your students enjoy the book!

Why Is Nonfiction Important?

Of the three types of text required in reading curricula—narrative, expository, and functional—many students lack enough successful experiences with expository (nonfiction) text. Part of the problem may be that they don't have the tools to navigate nonfiction and extract meaning from it. Some researchers have even suggested that the "fourth-grade slump" experienced by many students might be lessened if these children were exposed to more nonfiction in the elementary grades (Chall, Jacobs, and Baldwin, 1990; Duke, 2000). This includes not only having more nonfiction books in the classroom, but also being taught the tools to gain access to the information they contain. Interestingly, recent research has confirmed that some students actually prefer this type of text, so we see the motivation already exists. This certainly is one reason why nonfiction is important in the elementary grades. Other reasons include:

✔ **The ability to understand and write nonfiction is essential for school achievement.** Students encounter increasing amounts of nonfiction as they move through the grades. Their ability to find their way through the multiple features of this text and comprehend it is critical to reading progress.

✔ **High-stakes tests contain loads of nonfiction.** Recent standardized tests that affect students' promotion, graduation, and college acceptance contain approximately 50% reading tasks with nonfiction.

✔ **Reading nonfiction increases world knowledge and language that students don't have access to in daily conversations.** A student's understanding of the vocabulary in a text is highly correlated to his or her comprehension of that text. In addition, higher levels of background knowledge (acquired through wide reading and classroom discussions) are associated with higher comprehension of texts.

✔ **Understanding nonfiction helps to meet the increasing real-world literacy demands.** Recent NAEP (National Assessment of Educational Progress) studies have shown that high school students are graduating at alarming rates without the basic literacy skills required in today's job market. The 1990 U.S. Department of Labor SCANS report recommended that schools help students develop the workplace competencies necessary for today's job demands. These competencies include the ability to use and obtain information from the Internet. Approximately 96% of the text on the Web is informational (Kamil and Lane, 1998).

✔ **Nonfiction is the preferred reading material of many children.** Many kids in our schools are attracted to nonfiction text. The inclusion of more nonfiction in the curriculum for these "Info-Kids" may improve attitudes toward reading and serve as a catalyst for overall literacy growth (Caswell and Duke, 1998; Palmer and Stewart, 2003).

Characteristics of Nonfiction

One approach to teaching students how to read nonfiction—such as content area textbooks—is to build students' skills in identifying and using the various characteristics found in this type of text. For example:

- learning to **preview** the title, headings, and subheadings in a chapter of social studies text will enable the student to anticipate the main ideas that will be covered.

- knowing how to use **text features** (see a list of these graphic aids below) will allow the reader to take additional meaning from them rather than viewing them as a disruption to the flow of the text. In addition, it will help students integrate this information with that provided by the text.

    The following are common text features students will encounter in their science and social studies textbooks.

Diagrams	**Graphs**
Cycle diagrams	**Maps**
Flow charts	**Time lines**
Online sources	**Primary sources**
Text with multiple features	

- identifying the **text structures**, or organizational pattern within the text, will promote students' understanding and retention. Is the author comparing and contrasting life on the frontier with life in the cities? Is the text describing the physical characteristics of carnivorous dinosaurs?

    Five kinds of text structures, or patterns of organization, are commonly found in informational texts. These include the following:

    Description or listing Provides information, such as facts, characteristics, and attributes about a subject, event, person or concept. This organization is the most common pattern found in textbooks.

    Sequence or time order Presents a series of events that take place in a chronological order. The author traces the sequence or the steps in the process.

    Compare and contrast Points out the likenesses and/or differences between two or more subjects.

    Cause and effect Attempts to explain why something happens; how facts or events (causes) lead to other facts or events (effects). A single cause often has several effects. Also, a single event may have several causes.

    Problem and solution Describes a problem and presents one or more solutions to that problem.

How to Use This Book

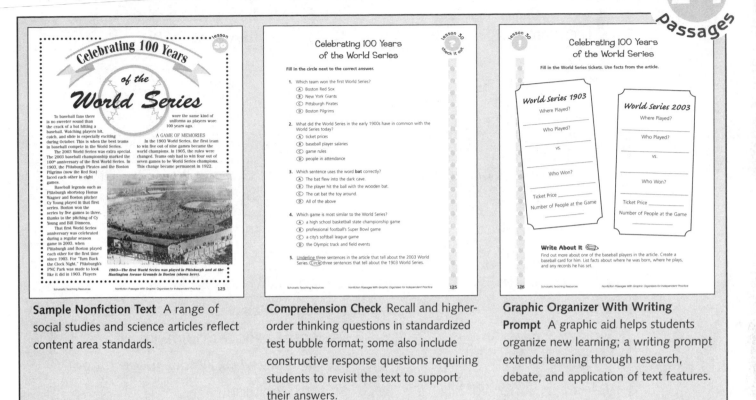

Sample Nonfiction Text A range of social studies and science articles reflect content area standards.

Comprehension Check Recall and higher-order thinking questions in standardized test bubble format; some also include constructive response questions requiring students to revisit the text to support their answers.

Graphic Organizer With Writing Prompt A graphic aid helps students organize new learning; a writing prompt extends learning through research, debate, and application of text features.

There are many ways we have used the passages in this book. How *you* use them will depend on your teaching style, student needs, schedule, and local curriculum requirements. Here's one management routine that has worked for us.

STEP 1 Distribute photocopies of the selected article, comprehension questions, and graphic organizer. You may wish to march through the articles in the order presented, or use articles related to topics being covered in your regular science and social studies curriculum. Distribute the article on Monday of each week.

STEP 2 Allow the students the entire week to complete the sequence of the lesson. We suggest the following for students:

Monday: Take home the article, read it, and answer the comprehension questions.
Tuesday: Reread the article and complete the graphic organizer.
Wednesday: Complete the writing assignment that follows the graphic organizer.
Thursday: Read the article and writing assignment to a family member. Have the family member sign the page to acknowledge student's completion of it.
Friday: Return the graphic organizer and writing assignment to you.

STEP 3 Review the answers to the comprehension questions as students grade their own papers. Collect the papers and record students' scores.

Content Area Standards Correlation

SELECTION TITLE	CONTENT AREA STANDARD
Go, Animals!	Science: Animal Families
From Grapevine to Jelly Jar	Social Studies: Factories and Agriculture
Creature Feature	Social Studies: Occupations
Bat at Night	Science: Animals
One Language, Many Nations	Social Studies: Multicultural Education
Seeds on the Go	Science: Plants
8 Reasons to Love an Octopus	Science: Animal Bodies
Pilgrim Children	Social Studies: U.S. History, Colonial Times
How Spiders Use Silk	Science: Animals
Hot Spot	Science: Volcanoes
Animal Survival	Science: Animal Adaptations
Tooth Truth	Social Studies: U.S. History, Government
Penguins of the World	Science: Animals
Stamp of Excellence	Social Studies: Special Needs Populations
Zoos Help Out!	Science: Endangered Animals
Chinese New Year	Social Studies: Understanding Cultures
Horsing Around	Social Studies: Special Needs Populations
Making Crayons	Social Studies: Factories and Manufacturing
A Chief in the Family	Social Studies: Native Americans
Digging Bones	Science: Human Body, Skeletons
Care for Our Earth!	Science: Ecology
Blast-Off!	Science: Machines
Sew Many Secrets	Social Studies: U.S. History, Slavery
Dinner Time!	Science: Animal Adaptations
House With a Trunk	Social Studies: Homes
Our Presidential Past	Social Studies: U.S. History, Character
Critters Cry for Help	Science: Endangered Animals
Could Your Body Go to Mars?	Science: Space
Spinning for a Good Cause	Science: Sports, Motion
Celebrating 100 Years of the World Series	Social Studies: U.S. History, Sports

Go, Animals!

In autumn, many different animals migrate, or move from one home to another. They go south, where it's warmer. Most animals stay together when they migrate. We have special names for these animal groups.

Go, Flock of Geese!

Geese migrate in a group called a **flock**. The flock flies in a V-shape. Different geese take turns leading the flock south.

Go, Herd of Caribou!

Caribou live in a big group called a **herd**. In autumn, the plants they eat start to die. That's when the whole herd leaves its home to find more food.

Go, Pod of Whales!

This is a **pod** of whales. In autumn, the water where they live can freeze. The pod swims south to warmer water. The young whales go, too. They eat enough food in the summer to last all autumn and winter. They won't eat again until spring!

Follow That Plane

Most cranes learn how to migrate from their parents. These cranes were way up north in Wisconsin. They needed to fly south to Florida. But something happened to the parents of the cranes in this photo, so they couldn't learn how to go. People taught the cranes to follow an airplane. The plane showed the flock the way to go!

WORD WISE

The word *migrate* has many relatives. How many of them do you know?

migrate (MY-grate) *verb* To move from one home to another.

migration (my-GRAY-shun) *noun* The movement from one home to another.

immigrant (IM-uh-gruhnt) *noun* A person who moves from one country to live in another country.

immigrate (IM-uh-grate) *verb* To move from one country to another country to live.

Go, Animals!

Fill in the circle next to the correct answer.

1. In the fall, some animals move from _____ .
   - (A) a warm place to a colder place
   - (B) a cold place to a warmer place
   - (C) the North Pole to the South Pole
   - (D) land to water

2. What causes caribou to move south in autumn?
   - (A) The plants they eat die in cold weather.
   - (B) The water they need freezes.
   - (C) They like to see new places.
   - (D) No one knows why.

3. Why might animals migrate in groups?
   - (A) They are safer from their enemies.
   - (B) They can keep warm.
   - (C) Only one animal knows the way.
   - (D) They can move faster.

4. Which sentence is correct?
   - (A) A pod of caribou can eat many plants.
   - (B) A flock of whales swam by our boat.
   - (C) A herd of geese landed on the pond.
   - (D) We saw a flock of cranes flying south.

5. In autumn, the whales leave the water that is near _____ .
   - (A) the North Pole
   - (B) Mexico
   - (C) Florida
   - (D) South America

Name the Group

For each kind of animal, write its group name.

ANIMAL NAME	GROUP NAME
geese	
caribou	
whales	
cranes	

Write About It ✏️

Find out the group names of these animals and any others: gorillas, lions, monkeys, giraffes, rhinoceroses, frogs, toads, ants, and grasshoppers.
You may be surprised by what you find! Add the names to the chart above or make your own chart.

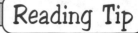

From Grapevine to Jelly Jar

Grape jelly isn't just mushed-up grapes. A lot has to happen to grapes before they become grape jelly. Follow the steps to see how grapes become jelly.

STEP 1: Pick Those Grapes

First, a farmer picks the grapes. Sometimes, farmers use machines to shake grapes off the vine. Then, the grapes go to a factory.

STEP 2: Crush Those Grapes

At the factory, the grapes are dumped into a machine called a **hopper**. The hopper crushes the grapes. It pushes them through a hole into a big pot.

STEP 3: Cook Those Grapes

The grapes are cooked in the big pot. They are mixed with sugar and grape juice. This makes the grape jelly thick and sweet.

STEP 4: Taste That Grape Jelly

Next, a person tastes a **sample**, or little bit, of the grape jelly. She makes sure it is sweet enough.

STEP 5: Fill Those Jelly Jars

Finally, a machine called a **filler** pours the jelly into jars. The jars are shipped all over the world to stores. People will buy the jelly and eat it. Yum!

From Grapevine to Jelly Jar

Fill in the circle next to the correct answer.

1. Which happens first?
   - Ⓐ A kid eats a jelly sandwich.
   - Ⓑ The jelly is put into jars at the factory.
   - Ⓒ The grapes are crushed.
   - Ⓓ Farmers pick grapes off the vine.

2. What is the name of the machine that pours the jelly into jars?
   - Ⓐ sample
   - Ⓑ hopper
   - Ⓒ filler
   - Ⓓ pot

3. Which of the following people work in the factory?
   - Ⓐ hopper
   - Ⓑ farmer
   - Ⓒ taster
   - Ⓓ driver

4. What would happen if sugar was not added to the cooking grapes?
   - Ⓐ The grape jelly would turn green.
   - Ⓑ The grape jelly would spoil.
   - Ⓒ The grape jelly would get too hard to eat.
   - Ⓓ The grape jelly would taste too sour.

5. List the people who help make grape jelly—from grapes on the vine to jelly jars in your home.

   _____

   _____

From Grapevine to Jelly Jar

The pictures below are out of order. Put them in order by numbering them from 1 to 6.

Second, the grapes are dumped into a hopper and crushed.

Next, a person tastes a sample of the grape jelly.

First, a farmer picks the grapes.

At last, the grape jelly is ready to eat. Yum!

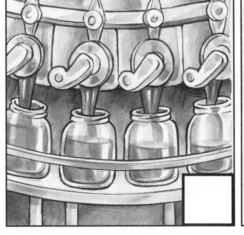

Then, the filler pours the grape jelly into jars.

Then, the grapes are cooked in a big pot.

Write About It

Write the steps in another process, such as making a sandwich, cooking a favorite dish, or building something.

Creature Feature

Gary Gero is wild about animals. He trained the cool creatures in the *Harry Potter and the Chamber of Secrets* movie. Recently, Gero spoke to *Scholastic News* about working with these animal actors.

Reading Tip

This article is an interview. It is written in question-and-answer format. The interviewer (*Scholastic News* editor) asks the questions. The animal trainer (Gary Gero) answers them. To help you, read the article with a partner. Have one person read the part of Gary Gero, and the other person read the part of the *Scholastic News* editor.

Gero has trained animals for almost 40 years. He says he has only been bitten once or twice. "If you get a bite, then you've made a mistake!" he says.

Scholastic News: How do you train the different animals?

Gary Gero: They're all trained the same way. They're given a toy or a treat when they do what they're supposed to.

Scholastic News: Owls are thought of as smart. Are they?

Gary Gero: Owls are not the brightest. An owl learns something after doing it a thousand times. It takes a raven or parrot only 10 times to learn the same thing.

Scholastic News: Are rats difficult to train?

Gary Gero: Rats are very intelligent. They learn simple things quickly. We trained them to go and stay in a certain spot and to retrieve (bring an object back).

Scholastic News: Were any of the actors on *Harry Potter* afraid of any of the animals?

Gary Gero: No. The kids were great. They all loved the animals.

Scholastic News: What advice do you have for kids interested in working with animals?

Gary Gero: Keep up your interest in animals, like your pets. And remember: It's very hard work, and the well-being of all the animals is in your hands.

Movie Animals as Pets

Animals that seem cute and cuddly in the movies may not be that way in real life. Which animals make great pets, and which ones are born to be wild?

Dalmatians were popular, or liked by many people, after the 1996 movie *101 Dalmatians*. In real life, many Dalmatians are nervous around kids.

Owls were bought as pets after the first Harry Potter movie. In real life, they need to be in the wild, so they do not make good pets.

Pug dogs became favorites after the *Men in Black II* movie came out. In real life, they are very good pets and love kids!

Creature Feature

Fill in the circle next to the correct answer.

1. Which of the following statements is <u>not</u> true?
   - Ⓐ Toys and treats are used to train animals.
   - Ⓑ Owls learn tricks very quickly.
   - Ⓒ Training animals is very hard work.
   - Ⓓ Rats can be trained to pick up small things.

2. Which animal makes the best pet for young children?
   - Ⓐ owl
   - Ⓑ Dalmatian
   - Ⓒ snake
   - Ⓓ pug dog

3. An **intelligent** animal is _____ .
   - Ⓐ fast
   - Ⓑ dumb
   - Ⓒ smart
   - Ⓓ well-trained

4. How is this article different from most magazine articles?
   - Ⓐ It has photographs.
   - Ⓑ It is written using questions and answers.
   - Ⓒ It is much longer than most articles.
   - Ⓓ It is about real people and events.

5. Which animal in the article is most interesting to you?_____
   <u>Underline</u> the sentences that tell about that animal.

Creature Feature

Complete the chart using facts from the article.

ANIMAL	FACTS LEARNED
owl	_____ _____ _____
rat	_____ _____ _____
Dalmatian	_____ _____ _____
pug dog	_____ _____ _____

Write About It

Write 3 more questions you would like to ask animal trainer Gary Gero.

1. _____ ?

2. _____ ?

3. _____ ?

Bat at Night

(1) *Night falls. The bat wakes up. What does the bat do at night?*

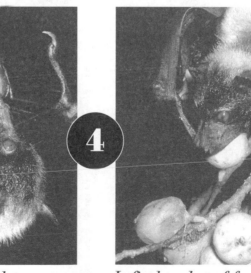

flying fox bat

(2) *When the sky gets dark, the bat gets ready to fly. It stretches its wings.*

(3) *The bat flies in the night sky. It looks for food. Like other nocturnal animals, this bat has big eyes to see in the dark.*

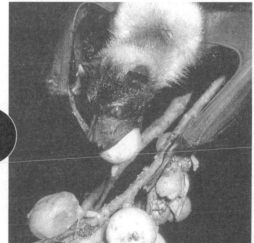

(4) *The bat finds food to eat.*

It finds a lot of fruit.

5

The bat also sips **nectar**, the sweet juice of flowers. The night is almost over.

6

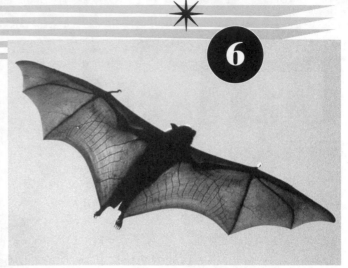

Day is coming. The bat flies back to its **roost**, the place where it sleeps.

7

Day is here. The bat goes to sleep. Bats hang upside down to sleep. Sleep tight!

WORD WISE

This guide will help you say and understand words in the article that you may not know.

nectar (NEK-tur) The sweet juice that is in flowers.

nocturnal (nok-TUR-nuhl) Animals that are awake at night.

roost (roost) The place where a bat sleeps.

More Bat Facts

Rodrigues fruit bat

Malayan flying fox

The bats in this picture are real. The one on the right is the biggest kind of bat in the world. Don't be scared though. Both bats are plant eaters. They eat mostly fruit.

Bat at Night

Fill in the circle next to the correct answer.

1. The article is about a _____ .
   - Ⓐ Stellaluna
   - Ⓑ Rodrigues fruit bat
   - Ⓒ flying fox bat
   - Ⓓ fruit bat

2. You can see a **nocturnal** animal _____ .
   - Ⓐ in the daytime
   - Ⓑ at night
   - Ⓒ at any time of day
   - Ⓓ only in the summer

3. What do nocturnal animals have in common?
   - Ⓐ They have big ears.
   - Ⓑ They see well in the dark.
   - Ⓒ They sleep when it's dark.
   - Ⓓ They live in trees.

4. Why do you think bats look for food at night?
   - Ⓐ Their enemies are asleep.
   - Ⓑ There is more fruit on the trees.
   - Ⓒ They fly better at night.
   - Ⓓ They don't see well.

5. Underline the two sentences in the article that tell what the bat eats. Then write the two things that the bat eats.

   _____

   _____

Bat at Night

Make a bat fact file. Write what the flying fox bat does in the daytime and what it does at night.

BAT IN THE DAYTIME

BAT AT NIGHT

_____

_____

_____

_____

_____

_____

_____

_____

_____

_____

_____

Write About It ✏️

There are hundreds of different kinds of bats. Some are the little brown bat, the big-eared bat, the long-nosed bat, and the flying fox. Get the facts about one of these bats. Make your own Fact File about the bat you choose.

ONE LANGUAGE, MANY NATIONS

What's in a name? When you say Latino, or Hispanic, there's more than you might think! Latinos come from many countries, each with its own history, traditions, foods, and way of life. However, these countries do share one thing: the Spanish language. That's because they were all settled by people who came from Spain hundreds of years ago. Read what these kids have to say about the countries where their families came from.

Cuba

Cuba is only 106 miles from Florida. It is the closest Caribbean island to the U.S. Over the last 40 years, many people have left Cuba to settle in Florida.

Dominican Republic

Many Dominicans have come to the U.S. to play baseball. One of them is homerun king Sammy Sosa!

Puerto Rico

The island of Puerto Rico is a commonwealth of the U.S. That means that Puerto Ricans are U.S. citizens. Their president is the same as ours. In Puerto Rico, people elect a governor, as in each state of the U.S.

Population Pie

The pie graph shows where the different Latino populations in the U.S. originated.

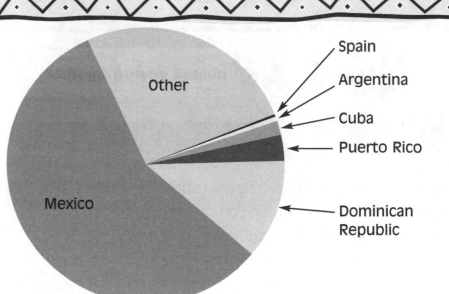

- Spain
- Argentina
- Cuba
- Puerto Rico
- Other
- Mexico
- Dominican Republic

Mexico

Mexico's capital, Mexico City, stands on the ruins of an ancient Aztec city. The Aztecs lived in Mexico long before Spanish explorers arrived 500 years ago.

Argentina

Argentina was once the land of the dinosaurs. The largest dinosaur ever discovered was found here. In 2001, a nest with thousands of dinosaur eggs was found. Move over, *Jurassic Park!*

Spain

Long ago, Spain was called Hispania, which means "land of rabbits." Ancient explorers gave it this name after finding a huge population of rabbits when they first visited the land.

One Language, Many Nations

Fill in the circle next to the correct answer.

1. Which country did baseball star Sammy Sosa come from?
   - (A) Cuba
   - (B) Spain
   - (C) Puerto Rico
   - (D) Dominican Republic

2. Which of the following is <u>not</u> a Spanish-speaking country?
   - (A) Cuba
   - (B) Argentina
   - (C) Japan
   - (D) Puerto Rico

3. The word **ancient** means the same as _____ .
   - (A) large
   - (B) very old
   - (C) settled
   - (D) land of rabbits

4. Which of the following countries is <u>not</u> an island?
   - (A) Cuba
   - (B) Puerto Rico
   - (C) Spain
   - (D) Dominican Republic

5. Circle one country on the map in the article. <u>Underline</u> the sentences in the article that tell about this country and its people.

One Language, Many Nations

Fill in the chart for one of the countries listed in the article.

COUNTRY NAME	LANGUAGE SPOKEN
_____	_____

Fact #1 _____

_____

_____

Fact #2 _____

_____

_____

Drawing of the country's shape

Write About It ✏️

Find out how to say the following words in Spanish.

hello _____   goodbye _____   one _____

thank you _____   yes _____   no _____

Seeds on the Go

When seeds travel, they move away from their parent plant. Now, they have a chance to find more water and room to sprout. Here are some ways seeds get around.

Seeds Blow in Wind!

The wind lifts dandelion seeds like parachutes. Then it takes them to new places where they can sprout into plants.

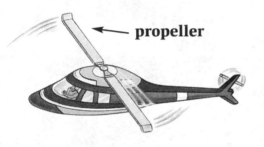

← **propeller**

Seeds Spin in Air!

These two maple seeds fall off the tree and spin in the wind. They work just like a **propeller**. The seeds spin away from their parent tree. Spinning helps the seeds travel farther than if they just fell.

Fact File

- A seed has a covering called a seed coat. This coat protects the seed.
- Food and a tiny plant are stored inside each seed. It is the tiny plant that grows, not the whole seed.
- If seeds just fell to the ground under their parent plant or tree, they would all sprout in the same place. There would not be enough water, sunlight, or minerals in the soil for all the plants. They would not get the things they need to grow.

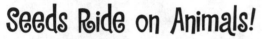

Seeds Float in Water!

This coconut is a big seed. It falls from a palm tree into the water. Then, the coconut floats like a boat on the water. (A coconut is light enough to float.) When the coconut gets to a beach, it can **sprout** into a new palm tree. Coconuts can float to a whole new island far away from their parent tree.

Seeds Ride on Animals!

This dog has **burs** on its fur. Tiny hooks all over the burs grab on to animal fur. The animal carries around the burs—and the tiny seeds inside the burs. Sooner or later, the animal scratches off the burs, or they fall to the ground on their own. Either way, the burs get a ride to a new place. Now, the seeds inside the burs can sprout into new plants.

Did You Know?

A man invented Velcro® after looking at a bur. The bur's hooks gave him the idea. One side of Velcro has tiny hooks, like a bur does. The other side has tiny loops. The hooks grab on to the loops and hold on!

Seeds on the Go!

Fill in the circle next to the correct answer.

1. Seeds travel to new places because _____ .
   - (A) otherwise animals might eat them
   - (B) they get big
   - (C) they fly like airplanes
   - (D) they need enough water and room to grow

2. Some seeds can travel far in the air because _____ .
   - (A) they are light
   - (B) they are heavy
   - (C) they are big
   - (D) they are sticky

3. What helps seeds travel from one place to another?
   - (A) wind
   - (B) water
   - (C) animals
   - (D) all of these things

4. The word **sprout** means _____ .
   - (A) begin to grow
   - (B) take a trip
   - (C) get wet
   - (D) spin

5. The main idea of the article is that _____ .
   - (A) seeds need water to grow
   - (B) some seeds spin in the air
   - (C) seeds travel and sprout away from their parent plant
   - (D) some seeds stick to the fur of animals

Seeds on the Go!

Look at each seed. Fill in the empty boxes to tell what the seed looks like and how it might travel.

KIND OF SEED	maple	dandelion	cocklebur
WHAT IT LOOKS LIKE	These seeds are shaped like a propeller.		
HOW IT MIGHT TRAVEL		These seeds blow in the wind like parachutes.	

Write About It

Imagine that you are a seed. Write about your travels to find a new place to grow. What was your parent plant? How did you get around? Where did you end up?

Nonfiction Passages With Graphic Organizers for Independent Practice

8 Reasons to Love an Octopus

It's easy to love an octopus. After all, an octopus is an awesome ocean animal. Just don't ask one to give you a hug!

1 An octopus has 8 arms. Count them. It uses its arms to swim and to catch meals.

2 An octopus has **suction cups** on the back of its arms. They help the octopus grab a meal, such as crabs, clams, and fish.

3 If an octopus loses an arm, it can grow another one! A starfish can do this too.

4 An octopus has no bones. Its body is soft and squishy. It can squeeze into small spaces. It can even squeeze into a seashell.

5 An octopus can change colors to **camouflage** (KAM-uh-flahzh), or blend in with its surroundings. It can also make its skin bumpy to look like rocks. That way, its enemies can't see it.

6 An octopus can **squirt** ink. It squirts ink at enemies. The enemies can't see the octopus through the ink. Then, the octopus swims away. This octopus thinks a human diver is an enemy.

7 Most octopuses are **nocturnal** (nok-TUR-nuhl), or awake at night. That's when they go hunting.

8 Octopus babies are cute. They have 8 tiny arms. That's the eighth reason to love an octopus. Could you love one?

Octopus Chart

NAME	WHAT IT LOOKS LIKE	SIZE	WHERE IT LIVES	COOL FACTS
North Pacific Giant Octopus		30 feet long (360 inches)	northern Pacific Ocean	This octopus can weigh 600 pounds! That's as much as a piano.
Common Octopus		15 to 28 inches long	all oceans	This octopus is great at changing colors.
Blue-Ringed Octopus		6 inches long	Pacific Ocean from Japan to Australia	This octopus has a poisonous bite. Watch out!

Nonfiction Passages With Graphic Organizers for Independent Practice

8 Reasons to Love an Octopus

Fill in the circle next to the correct answer.

1. How can an octopus protect itself from its enemies?
    - (A) It can change its color to match where it is.
    - (B) It can squirt ink in its enemy's face.
    - (C) It can make its skin look like a rock's surface.
    - (D) All of the above

2. How do you say the letter **c** in the word **ocean**?
    - (A) the same as the letter **k** in **kitten**
    - (B) the same as the letter **c** in **center**
    - (C) the same as the letters **ch** in **cheap**
    - (D) the same as the letters **sh** in **shoe**

3. A **nocturnal** animal _____ .
    - (A) lives in the ocean
    - (B) hides by blending in with its surroundings
    - (C) sleeps during the daytime
    - (D) has more than two legs

4. Which octopus is dangerous?
    - (A) Common Octopus
    - (B) Blue-Ringed Octopus
    - (C) North Pacific Giant Octopus
    - (D) All octopuses are dangerous.

5. Circle the words in the article that have pronunciations after them. What does each word mean?

    _____

    _____

8 Reasons to Love an Octopus

On each octopus arm, write one fact about this animal.

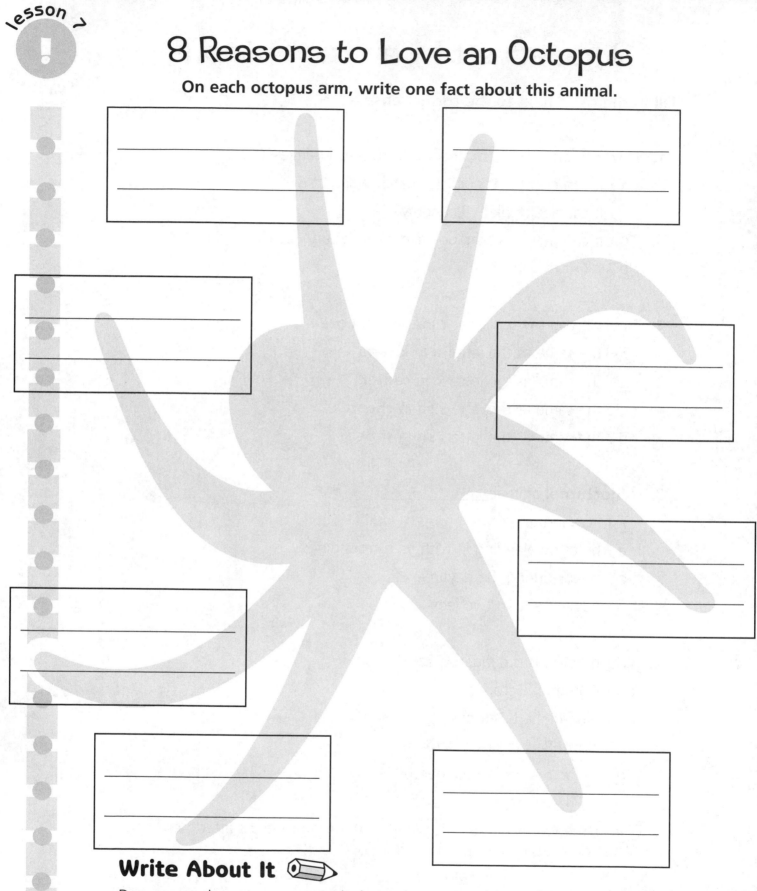

Write About It

Draw an underwater scene. Include an octopus and any other sea creatures you wish in the drawing. Write 2 or 3 sentences to tell about your picture.

Nonfiction Passages With Graphic Organizers for Independent Practice

Living the Pilgrim Life

The Pilgrims came to America in 1620. Read what life was like for Pilgrim children. As you read, compare your life to theirs.

lesson

8

PILGRIM CHILDREN

These children today are dressed like Pilgrims to help you imagine what life was like back then.

yoke

WORD WISE

- You may not know some of the words in the article. The photos will help you. For example, the **labels** show you what each piece of clothing is called.

- This **guide** will help you pronounce some of the words.
  breeches (BRICH-uhs)
  doublet (DUB-let)
  kindling (KINNED-ling)
  petticoat (PET-ee-coat)

Pilgrims did not have water in their homes. The children carried water from a stream with a yoke.

The children dressed like adults. The clothes are just like adult clothes. Children began to dress like this when they were 6 years old. They wore long sleeves, even in the summer!

The children did a lot of chores. All the Pilgrims had to work to live. Children did chores every day. The children cleaned the goat house and helped milk the goats. Children also gathered **kindling**, or firewood. They picked wild berries when they were ripe.

hat

doublet

waistcoat

apron

petticoat

breeches

stockings

The children played Pilgrim games. The children had time for fun, too. They even played games. This one is called "Troll My Dame." It is played with marbles. It's like mini bowling.

Living the Pilgrim Life

Fill in the circle next to the correct answer.

1. Which sentence is true?
    - Ⓐ Pilgrim children helped their families do work.
    - Ⓑ Pilgrim children had a lot of free time.
    - Ⓒ Pilgrim children lived just like children today.
    - Ⓓ Pilgrim children never played.

2. The Pilgrims got their food _____ .
    - Ⓐ from a supermarket
    - Ⓑ from England
    - Ⓒ by growing it and finding it in the wild
    - Ⓓ from the ships they came on

3. Pilgrim homes had no _____ .
    - Ⓐ walls
    - Ⓑ roofs
    - Ⓒ gardens
    - Ⓓ running water

4. Why did the Pilgrims need firewood?
    - Ⓐ to cook their food
    - Ⓑ to warm their homes
    - Ⓒ to boil water
    - Ⓓ for all these things

5. Write what we call some of the clothes Pilgrim children wore.

    What do we call a **doublet**? _____

    What do we call **breeches**? _____

    What do we call a **petticoat**? _____

    What do we call boys' **stockings**? _____

Then and Now

Compare your life with the life of Pilgrim children. Fill in the chart.
Tell at least one thing about clothing, chores, and games.

PILGRIM CHILDREN	YOU
Clothing _____	_____
_____	_____
_____	_____
_____	_____
Chores _____	_____
_____	_____
_____	_____
_____	_____
Games _____	_____
_____	_____
_____	_____
_____	_____

Write About It

Imagine that you are a Pilgrim child. Make two lists. In one list, write what
you would like about living in those days. In the other list, write what you
would miss from life today.

How Spiders Use Silk

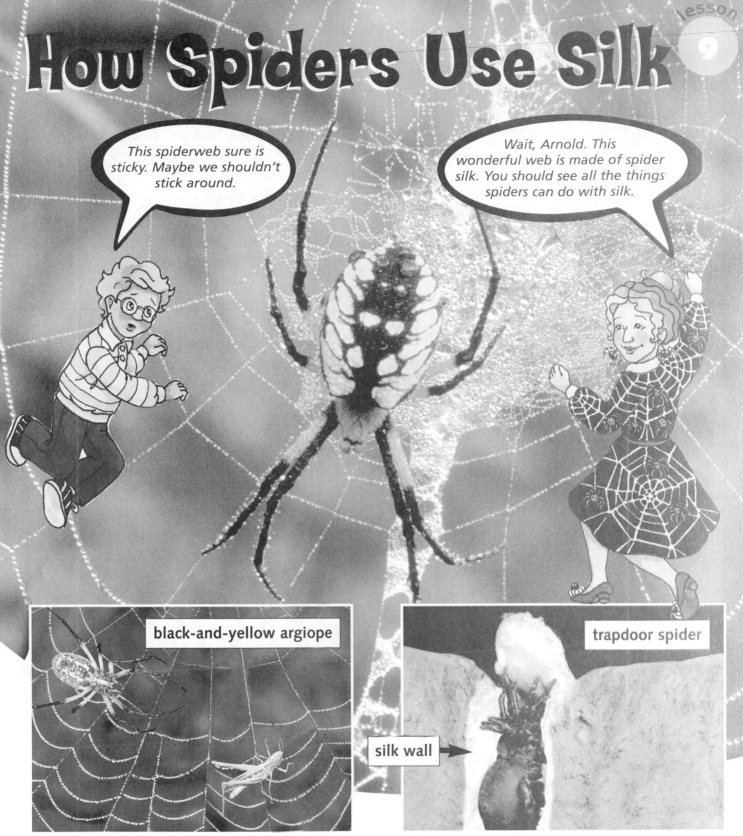

This spiderweb sure is sticky. Maybe we shouldn't stick around.

Wait, Arnold. This wonderful web is made of spider silk. You should see all the things spiders can do with silk.

black-and-yellow argiope

trapdoor spider

silk wall

Spiders Trap Food With Silk

This spider weaves a web with silk. A grasshopper jumped into the web and got caught.

Spiders Build Burrows With Silk

This spider lines its **burrow**, an underground home, with silk. The silk makes the walls of the burrow strong.

jumping spider

Spiders Make Safety Lines With Silk

This spider spins a line of silk as it jumps. If the spider falls, it can hang from its line of silk.

black widow

Spiders Keep Babies Safe in Silk

This spider weaves an egg sac with silk. The egg sac keeps the eggs safe. **Spiderlings** crawl out when they hatch.

Spiderlings Fly Away
by Keesha

Some spiderlings climb to a high place. Then they spin lines of silk. The wind blows the spiderlings, like balloons, to a new home. This is called **ballooning**.

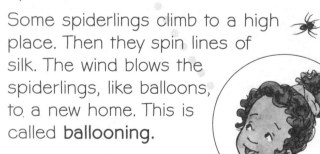

S I L K P O W E R

Spider silk is super strong. It stretches, too. So scientists like Randy Lewis want to use it in new ways.

"Spider silk could be used to make ropes, seat belts, and clothes for firefighters," says Dr. Lewis.

Spiders don't make enough silk for people to use, though. Dr. Lewis is finding out how scientists can make silk like spiders do.

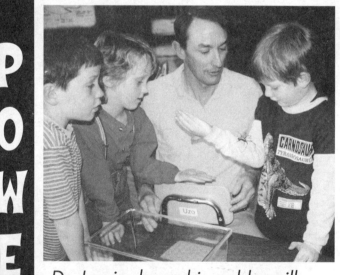

Dr. Lewis shows his golden silk spider to a class of second-graders and third-graders.

Spiders

Fill in the circle next to the correct answer.

1. Spiderlings are _____ .
   Ⓐ mother spiders
   Ⓑ grasshoppers
   Ⓒ baby spiders
   Ⓓ spider webs

2. How does the black widow spider's egg sac keep the eggs safe?
   Ⓐ Enemies cannot see the eggs to eat them.
   Ⓑ The baby spiders cannot get out.
   Ⓒ It's big.
   Ⓓ It's small.

3. Why do you think a spider's web is sticky?
   Ⓐ To keep trapped insects from falling off
   Ⓑ To help the web stay up
   Ⓒ Because it's made of silk
   Ⓓ Because it's made of gum

4. Which sentence is true?
   Ⓐ All spiders live above the ground.
   Ⓑ Some spiders live underground.
   Ⓒ Spiders cannot jump from one place to another.
   Ⓓ Spider silk is not strong.

5. Circle the names of four spiders in the article.

How Spiders Use Silk

In each part of the web, write one way that spiders use silk. Then add details about each way that spiders use silk.

SILK

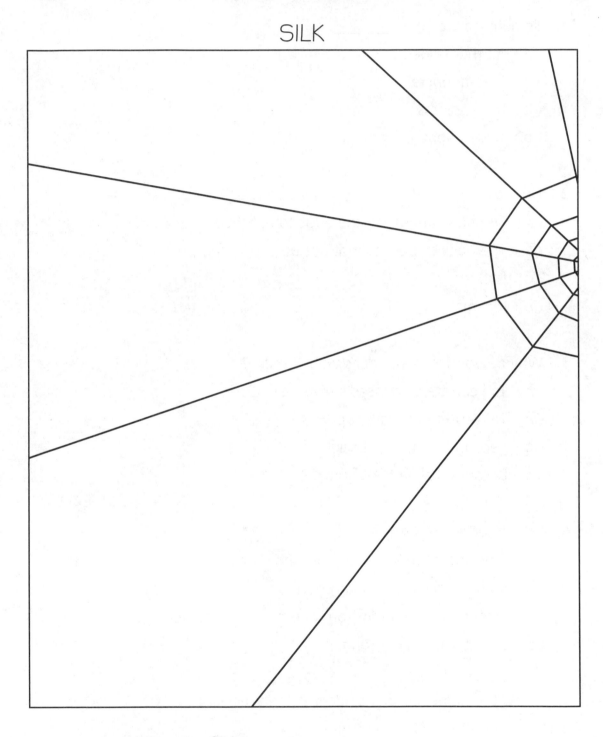

Write About It!

If you could make silk like a spider, what would you make? Why?

Hot Spot

Vesuvius last erupted in 1944. People live near the volcano because the soil is rich and good for growing crops such as grapes, tomatoes, onions, oranges, and lemons.

The people who live near Italy's Mount Vesuvius (veh-SOO-vee-uhs) must be ready to leave the area at any time. Why? Vesuvius, a huge volcano, may soon erupt, or explode. That means big trouble for those people—all 2 million of them!

Fire From the Mountain

If Vesuvius erupts, it will release hot gases, thick ashes, and lava, or red-hot liquid rock. It will be very dangerous for anyone to be nearby. "We expect that a large area could be destroyed in a few minutes," says Edoardo Del Pezzo, a volcano expert. This is what happened almost 2,000 years ago. An eruption by Vesuvius buried the ancient, or very old, city of Pompeii (pom-PAY).

Escaping the Eruption

To make sure everyone can get to safety, special practice drills are held. When sirens are sounded, the people get to their cars quickly and drive away from the area.

Scientists are studying Vesuvius closely. They hope to know when the volcano will erupt before it happens. But Del Pezzo says, "It is not possible to actually know when it will erupt."

How a Volcano Erupts

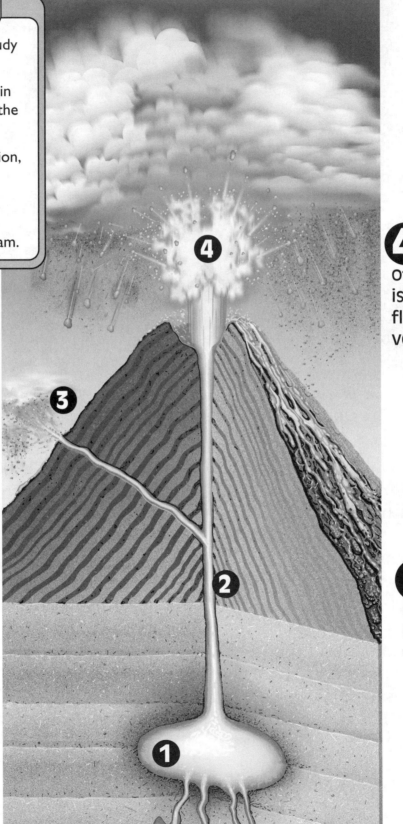

4 After magma bursts out of the volcano it is called lava. Lava flows down the volcano's sides.

3 Hot magma bursts through holes in the Earth, called vents. Ash, gases, and rocks also blast into the sky.

2 Pressure builds even more inside the volcano.

1 Magma is hot liquid rock that collects in a pool under the Earth's crust. It pushes up into the volcano.

Hot Spot

Fill in the circle next to the correct answer.

1. Where is Mount Vesuvius?

   (A) in the United States

   (B) in the city of Pompeii

   (C) in Italy

   (D) in the mountains of Venezuela

2. Which of the following words rhymes with **Pompeii**?

   (A) tree

   (B) play

   (C) radio

   (D) people

3. Hot liquid rock inside the Earth is called _____ .

   (A) lava

   (B) volcano

   (C) eruption

   (D) magma

4. Who is helped by living near Mount Vesuvius?

   (A) farmers

   (B) old people

   (C) scientists

   (D) skiers

5. Underline three sentences in the article that tell about Mount Vesuvius.

Hot Spot

Make your own diagram of a volcano erupting. Use the facts in the article to label your drawing.

Write About It ✎

Learn more about volcanoes. Read about another famous volcano, such as Mount St. Helens (United States), Paricutin (Mexico), Cotopaxi (Ecuador), Krakatau (Indonesia), Mount Pinatubo (Philippines), or Mount Etna (Italy).

Animal Survival

All animals need food, water, oxygen, safe shelter, and the right body temperature to stay alive. Some animals have special body parts that help them meet their need for food, water, and the right body temperature.

Reading Tip

Before you read, preview the article. Here's how:

- Read the title and the headings.
- Look at the photos.
- Read the introduction.
- Say to yourself, "This article will be about . . ."
- After you read, see if your predictions were correct.

Food

Many animals have special mouth or head parts that help them get food. For example, this woodpecker uses its long beak to get under a tree's bark. Then it can eat the bugs that live there.

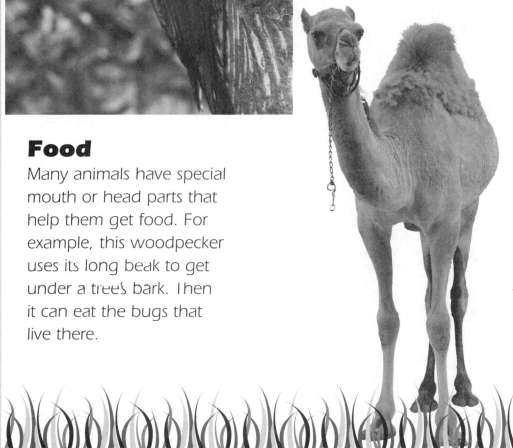

Water

Some animals have special body parts that help them get water. The camel, for example, does not sweat much even in desert heat. This is because it saves water in its tissues, which are cells that form part of the body. That is why a camel can go without drinking water for nearly a month.

Temperature

Some animals have long coats that keep them warm in cold temperatures. The yak lives high in the mountains in Tibet, a country in Asia. It needs its woolly coat to keep warm.

Did You Know? An elephant uses its trunk to feed itself, squirt water in its mouth, and spray itself with cool water.

Animal Survival

Fill in the circle next to the best answer.

1. Special mouth or head parts help some animals _____ .
   - Ⓐ sleep at night
   - Ⓑ get food
   - Ⓒ hide from their enemies
   - Ⓓ stay warm

2. It's important for a camel to save water in its body because _____ .
   - Ⓐ it lives in the desert, where there is little water to drink
   - Ⓑ it never gets thirsty
   - Ⓒ it only likes to drink water once in a while
   - Ⓓ it doesn't need water to live

3. Yaks live in a place that is _____ .
   - Ⓐ warm
   - Ⓑ hot and wet
   - Ⓒ a jungle
   - Ⓓ cold

4. A tree's **bark** is its _____ .
   - Ⓐ branches
   - Ⓑ covering
   - Ⓒ sound
   - Ⓓ leaves

5. Find the sentence in the article that tells three ways an elephant's trunk helps the elephant survive. Write the three ways here.

   1. _____

   2. _____

   3. _____

What Does It Do?

Complete the chart using facts from the article.

ANIMAL	BODY PART	WHAT IT DOES
woodpecker	_____	_____
	_____	_____
camel	_____	_____
	_____	_____
yak	_____	_____
	_____	_____
elephant	_____	_____
	_____	_____
_____	_____	_____
	_____	_____
_____	_____	_____
	_____	_____

Write About It ✏️

Find out about other animals, such as a bat, an anteater, or a giraffe, with body parts that help them meet their needs. Add the information to the chart.

TOOTH TRUTH

President Washington rarely smiled. He kept his lips sealed to hide his teeth. Washington wore a pair of dentures (DEN-churz), or false teeth. These dentures were uncomfortable for Washington, but they looked better than his natural smile. Washington had only one of his own teeth left!

February is Dental Health Month. If you want to keep all of your teeth, you have to take proper care of them. To save your smile, be sure to brush your teeth twice a day, floss regularly, and visit the dentist twice a year.

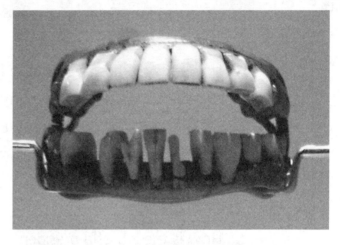

Many people think that Washington wore wooden teeth. They were really made of cow and hippo teeth, ivory, and lead.

NO KING FOR U.S.

Some people wanted President Washington to be King of the United States. Washington refused. He believed in a system of government where the people vote for their leaders.

Shortly after the Revolutionary War, some of Washington's army officers offered to help him take over our new nation. Washington disagreed with these men. He said, "banish (get rid of) these thoughts from your mind." Finally, an election was held, and Washington became our first president, instead of a king. Look at the chart below to find out the differences between a king and a president.

KING   VS.   PRESIDENT

KING	PRESIDENT
• Born into the position	• Elected by the people
• Works alone to make decisions	• Works with others to make decisions
• Cannot be voted out of office	• Can be voted out of office
• Has the job for life	• Elected to a four-year term

Tooth Truth

Fill in the circle next to the correct answer.

1. How can you keep your teeth healthy?
   - (A) go to the dentist two times a year
   - (B) floss every night before going to bed
   - (C) brush your teeth at least two times a day
   - (D) All of the above

2. How is the job of a president the same as that of a king?
   - (A) Both have the job as long as they want.
   - (B) Both are elected by the people in their countries.
   - (C) Both make laws for the people in their countries.
   - (D) Both work by themselves to make laws.

3. Another word for **nation** is _____ .
   - (A) king
   - (B) health
   - (C) denture
   - (D) country

4. What were George Washington's teeth made of?
   - (A) wood
   - (B) pearls
   - (C) hippo teeth
   - (D) elephant teeth

5. Underline the sentences in the article that tell how to take care of your teeth.

Tooth Truth

Make a Dental Health poster. List the ways to keep your teeth healthy. Add drawings to your poster.

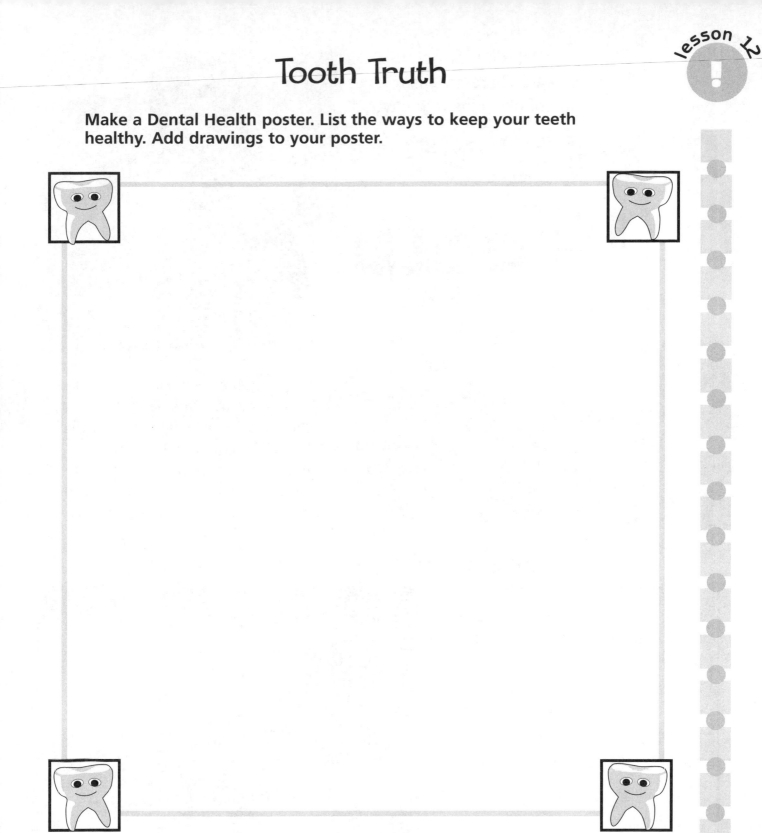

Write About It

Learn more about George Washington. Find a book about him. List 5 facts you learn from the book. Share them with your class.

Believe it or not, this is a penguin! There are many kinds of penguins in the world!

PENGUINS of the WORLD

North
West — East
South

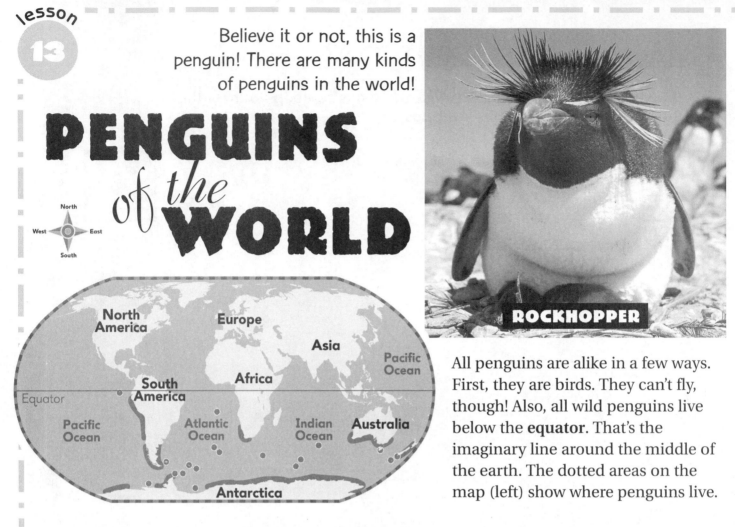

ROCKHOPPER

All penguins are alike in a few ways. First, they are birds. They can't fly, though! Also, all wild penguins live below the **equator**. That's the imaginary line around the middle of the earth. The dotted areas on the map (left) show where penguins live.

Let's learn about different kinds of penguins.

ROCKHOPPER

What They Look Like: Rockhoppers have a yellow crest, or bunch of feathers, on their heads.

Habitat: They live on islands with tall grasses and rocky cliffs.

Fun Fact: They hop up and down rocks, just like their name says.

The • shows where rockhoppers live.

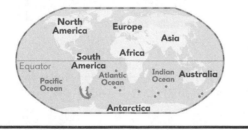

EMPEROR

What They Look Like: Emperors have a black head and back. Their chest is yellow and white.

Habitat: They live on the Antarctic ice and in the waters around Antarctica.

Fun Fact: These are the biggest penguins. They are about as tall as a 6-year-old child.

In winter, the female emperor penguin lays one egg. The male takes care of the egg. He balances it on the tops of his feet for about two months, until the egg hatches.

The • shows where emperors live.

LITTLE BLUE

What They Look Like: Little blues have a blue back and a white belly.

Habitat: They live on the sandy beaches of Australia and New Zealand.

Fun Fact: These are the smallest penguins of all. These little penguins only come up to a child's knee.

The • shows where little blues live.

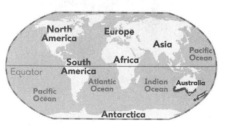

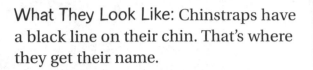

What They Look Like: Chinstraps have a black line on their chin. That's where they get their name.

Habitat: They live on icebergs and rocky islands near Antarctica.

Fun Fact: They stamp their feet when they are angry.

The • shows where chinstraps live.

What They Look Like: Africans have a black stripe around their chest and pink above their eyes.

Habitat: They live on beaches in South Africa and nearby.

Fun Fact: Their call sounds like a donkey—*hee-haw!*

The • shows where Africans live.

Penguins of the World

Fill in the circle next to the correct answer.

1. Which penguin got its name from something it does?

   (A) Little Blue

   (B) Emperor

   (C) Rockhopper

   (D) Chinstrap

2. Which sentence is true?

   (A) Some penguins live at the North Pole.

   (B) Some penguins can fly.

   (C) All penguins live in Antarctica.

   (D) All penguins live south of the equator.

3. How are all penguins alike?

   (A) They all live near water.

   (B) They are all the same color.

   (C) They all live in very cold places.

   (D) They are all the same size.

4. An animal's **habitat** is _____ .

   (A) what it eats

   (B) how it looks

   (C) where it lives

   (D) the sound it makes

5. Find two penguins in the article whose names tell how they look.
   Circle the names. Underline the sentences that tells how
   they look.

Penguins of the World

Tip:
Reread the beginning of the article to find out how all penguins are alike.

Choose two of the penguins you read about. Fill in the graphic organizer to show how they are same and how they are different.

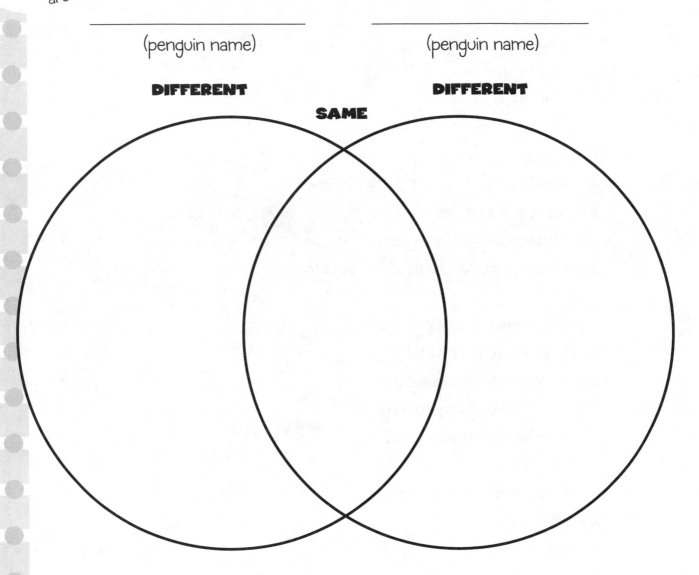

_____
(penguin name)

_____
(penguin name)

DIFFERENT   **SAME**   **DIFFERENT**

Write About It

Describe three interesting facts you learned from the article. Tell why you think they are interesting.

1. _____

2. _____

3. _____

STAMP
of
EXCELLENCE

The United States Postal Service shows its Olympic spirit. This agency issued, or put out, a stamp to honor the Special Olympics.

The Special Olympics is a sporting event in which mentally disabled people take part.

The Special Olympics was started by Eunice Kennedy Shriver. Eunice was President John F. Kennedy's sister. One of their other sisters, Rosemary, was born with mental retardation. A person with mental retardation learns more slowly than other people his or her age. Eunice saw the big challenges her sister faced. So, she wanted a competition in which people with mental disabilities could show their athletic skills.

The first Special Olympics was held in 1968 in Chicago, Illinois. About 1,000 athletes competed in three events: athletics, floor hockey, and aquatics. Today, about 1,000,000 athletes from 160 countries compete in 26 sports.

In 2003, the Special Olympics World Summer Games took place in Ireland from June 21 to June 29. There were many events, including soccer, basketball, swimming, and gymnastics.

The U.S. Postal Service hopes the stamp will make more people aware of this important event.

The Special Olympics stamp costs 80 cents. It can be used for packages mailed to places outside the U.S.

Stamp of Excellence

Fill in the circle next to the correct answer.

1. When did the Special Olympics start?
   - (A) 1868
   - (B) 1965
   - (C) 1968
   - (D) 1999

2. Which sports are played in the Special Olympics?
   - (A) soccer
   - (B) gymnastics
   - (C) basketball
   - (D) all of the above

3. Which sport is played during **aquatic** events?
   - (A) floor hockey
   - (B) swimming
   - (C) athletics
   - (D) baseball

4. Which of the following is <u>not</u> on the Special Olympics stamp?
   - (A) medal
   - (B) athlete
   - (C) price
   - (D) photograph

5. List three facts you learned from the article.

   _____

   _____

   _____

Stamp of Excellence

Create your own stamp for the Special Olympics. Write 2 or 3 sentences to describe your stamp.

_____

_____

_____

Write About It ✏️

Write a letter to a friend inviting him or her to go to the Special Olympics with you. Tell them about this important event. List the sporting activities you are most interested in seeing.

ZOOS HELP OUT!

Not many golden lion tamarins are left in the world. They are endangered, or close to dying out forever. Zoos want these monkeys to be around for a long time. They take good care of the tamarins they have.

Zoos help their tamarins stay healthy. They found out that eating insects is good for tamarins. This tamarin just ate a cricket. Crunch!

Zoos help raise baby tamarins. They make sure the babies born there get good care. Some babies need extra help. This baby needed a bottle.

Zoos help their tamarins get exercise. They give them lots of trees and branches to climb on. Sometimes, the zookeepers move the branches around. That makes climbing more fun! Zoos bring some of their tamarins back to the wild. They let them go in the rain forest of Brazil. One day, the forest may be full of these monkeys again.

Thank you, zoos!

Reading Tip

As you read, stop and study the bar graph.

- Read the title to find out the topic of the graph.
- Look at each label. Think about what the numbers stand for.
- To read the graph, use your finger to trace from the top of the bar to the number on the left.
- Think about the comparisons the graph is making.

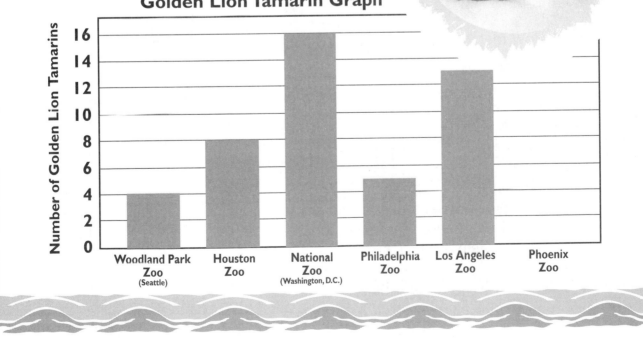

Golden Lion Tamarin Graph

Number of Golden Lion Tamarins

16 14 12 10 8 6 4 2 0

Woodland Park Zoo (Seattle) — Houston Zoo — National Zoo (Washington, D.C.) — Philadelphia Zoo — Los Angeles Zoo — Phoenix Zoo

Zoos Help Out!

Fill in the circle next to the correct answer.

1. The zoo in which city has the most golden lion tamarins?
   - (A) Los Angeles
   - (B) Philadelphia
   - (C) Washington, D.C.
   - (D) Phoenix

2. How are zoos helping to save tamarins?
   - (A) They return healthy tamarins to the rain forest.
   - (B) They raise tamarins to increase their numbers.
   - (C) They keep the tamarins healthy and well-fed.
   - (D) All of the above

3. Which word means the same as **close to dying out**?
   - (A) dangerous
   - (B) entrapped
   - (C) extinct
   - (D) endangered

4. How many golden lion tamarins are in the Houston Zoo?
   - (A) 0
   - (B) 4
   - (C) 8
   - (D) 16

5. Underline the sentences in the article that tell what zoos have done to help the tamarins. Circle the sentence that tells why the tamarins needed help.

Zoos Help Out!

Draw a picture of a tamarin monkey. List three facts you learned about this animal.

Fact #1 _____

_____

Fact #2 _____

_____

Fact #3 _____

_____

Write About It ✏️

Find out about another endangered animal, such as the giant panda, blue whale, rhinoceros, tiger, or orangutan. Write what is being done to help this animal.

CHINESE NEW YEAR

MAY YOU PROSPER!

Gung Hay Fat Choy! May you prosper! This is the Chinese greeting for the New Year. In China, New Year is the most important holiday. It is celebrated by Chinese people all over the world.

The date of Chinese New Year is not January 1. In fact, the New Year begins on a different day each year. It is sometime between January 21 and February 19. Why is that? The Chinese calendar is based on the **phases** of the moon. These phases are changes in the moon's shape as it looks to us from Earth.

Chinese New Year begins when the moon is in the "new moon" phase. During this phase, the moon cannot be seen. The celebrations end 15 days later, when the full moon lights the sky.

Fact File

- Before the Chinese New Year celebration, people cut their hair, wash their clothes, buy new clothes, and clean their homes. People do this to say goodbye to the old year and start the new year fresh.

- People decorate their homes with flowers, trays of candy, and good luck poems written on red paper. Red is the color for good luck.

- During the holiday, families and friends give each other gifts such as oranges and tangerines. These fruits stand for good luck and wealth.

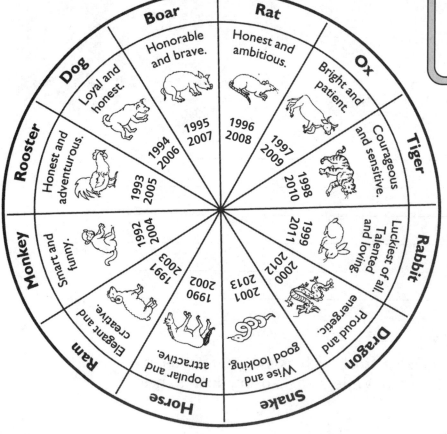

Each year on the Chinese calendar is named for 1 of 12 animals. The chart shows the animals and the years they represent.

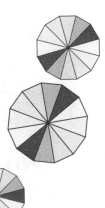

Chinese New Year in the U.S.

Los Angeles, California

Los Angeles has had a Chinese New Year parade every year for 104 years! A huge painted dragon, swaying back and forth, starts off the parade. The dragon is the symbol of power, luck, strength, and success. It is followed by floats, marching bands, and drummers. People from all over the country come to the colorful parade. It's easy to see why!

This family has a feast at home for Chinese New Year. Notice the oranges and tangerines, which stand for luck and wealth.

Chicago, Illinois

On New Year's eve, the night before New Year's day, houses are brightly lit and a large family dinner is served. Popular dishes are duck, dumplings, and fish. Many people stay up until midnight, when fireworks are lit. New Year's day is spent visiting family and friends.

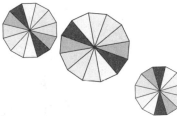

Connie puts her finger in a ring under each handkerchief. Look at them spin!

Portland, Maine

Portland celebrates Chinese New Year with a fair. Children show their talents. Here, Connie spins handkerchiefs on her fingers. "It's traditional," she said. "I learned how in China." Connie lived in China before her family moved to Maine.

People at the fair learn about Chinese **culture**, or the Chinese way of life. They will hear Chinese music, play Chinese games, and eat Chinese food.

Chinese New Year

Fill in the circle next to the correct answer.

1. Chinese New Year begins _____ .

    Ⓐ January 1

    Ⓑ in December

    Ⓒ on a different day each year

    Ⓓ on the same day each year

2. The word **culture** describes a people's _____ .

    Ⓐ music, art, foods, and celebrations

    Ⓑ birthdays

    Ⓒ country where they were born

    Ⓓ calendar

3. Which one of these is a symbol of strength to the Chinese?

    Ⓐ oranges and tangerines

    Ⓑ the color red

    Ⓒ duck

    Ⓓ dragon

4. The eve of your birthday would be _____ .

    Ⓐ the night before your birthday

    Ⓑ the same night as your birthday

    Ⓒ the day after your birthday

    Ⓓ the week of your birthday

5. Use the Chinese New Year chart to answer these questions.

    What animal is the symbol for this year? _____

    In which year will the tiger be the Chinese New Year symbol? _____

    Which animal will be the symbol sooner—the horse or the rabbit?

    _____

Chinese New Year

People who move to a new country often bring their celebrations, foods, and traditions with them. Fill in the chart to show how people in the United States celebrate the Chinese New Year holiday.

DECORATIONS	
FOOD	
SYMBOLS	
ACTIVITIES	

Write About It

Write about your favorite holiday. When is it? Why is it your favorite? How do you celebrate it? What special foods do you have?

Horsing Around

When it comes to guiding blind people from place to place, it's no longer just a dog's world. Pygmy horses are now on the job, too. They're proving that tiny horses can be a big help to people in need.

Guide horses do not lose their cool when they see people or cars. Staying calm helps them guide their owners safely. Guide horses must be fitted with tennis shoes. Otherwise, their hooves may cause them to slip on hardwood floors.

Small Wonder

Pygmy horses are **miniature**, or little, horses born with short legs. In fact, their legs are so short that the horses only grow to about two feet tall. A regular horse grows to about five feet tall. The small size of pygmy horses makes it easy for them to pass through doors, or get into elevators and cars.

Practice Makes Perfect

Guide horses are trained at the Guide Horse Foundation in North Carolina. Janet Burleson is one of the owners and horse trainers at the foundation.

"It takes about nine months for a horse to learn how to help blind people," Burleson says. During that time, the horses learn **commands** like "forward," "back," and "stop." They also learn how to walk with an owner, and to avoid obstacles, or things that get in the way.

The horses spend two weeks in training with their blind owners before moving in with them. "We have found homes for two guide horses," Burleson says, "and the owners couldn't be happier."

Guide Dog vs. Guide Horse

Dogs and pygmy horses are two animal species trained to guide blind people. Here's how they compare.

	GUIDE DOG	GUIDE HORSE
life span	10 to 12 years	30 to 40 years
food	Dog food	Grass and oats
vision	Can see very well at night; has eyes at the front of its head—allows the dog to see things in front of it.	Can see very well at night; has eyes on the side of its head—allows the horse to see things in front and on its sides.
home life	Lives indoors, and does not need a backyard	Lives indoors, but needs a backyard where it can eat grass

Horsing Around

Fill in the circle next to the correct answer.

1. How long does it take to train a guide horse?
    - Ⓐ two weeks
    - Ⓑ one month
    - Ⓒ nine months
    - Ⓓ one year

2. What do a guide dog and guide horse have in common?
    - Ⓐ They both live to be over 20 years old.
    - Ⓑ They both live inside homes.
    - Ⓒ They both have trouble seeing at night.
    - Ⓓ They both wear special shoes.

3. Which word means the same as **small**?
    - Ⓐ little
    - Ⓑ miniature
    - Ⓒ tiny
    - Ⓓ all of the above

4. Which part of the body is used for **vision**?
    - Ⓐ legs
    - Ⓑ stomach
    - Ⓒ eyes
    - Ⓓ back

5. List three facts about pygmy horses that you learned from the article.

    _____

    _____

    _____

Horsing Around

Complete the graphic organizer below. Write how a guide dog and a guide horse are alike and different.

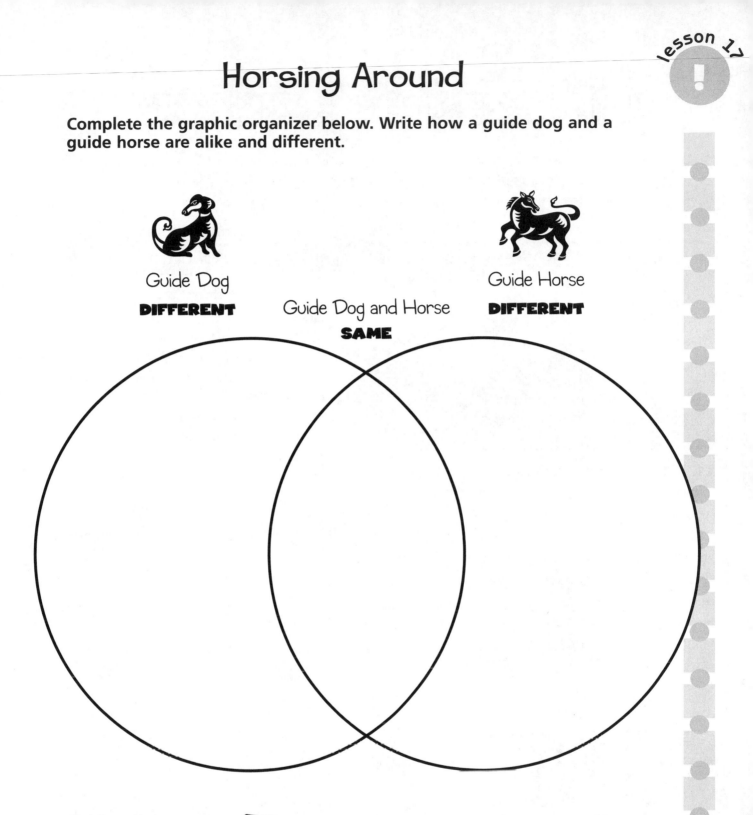

Guide Dog
DIFFERENT

Guide Dog and Horse
SAME

Guide Horse
DIFFERENT

Write About It

Find out about other animals that help people. These include dogs, cats, horses, monkeys, and rabbits. Pick one animal and learn more about how it is trained to help people.

MAKING CRAYONS

Do you ever wonder where crayons come from? They are made in a **factory**. A factory (FAK-tuh-ree) is a building where things are made in large numbers. Machines usually help make the things. Find out how crayons are made, step by step.

STEP 1 Crayons are made from wax. At the crayon factory, the wax is melted. Then, it is mixed with colored powder.

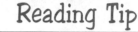
Reading Tip

This article shows you the **sequence**, or the steps, in making crayons.

• Read the steps in order.

• Start with Step **1**. After you read, look carefully at the photo. Read the caption, too.

• Then read Step **2**. Look at the photo and read the caption.

• Keep going in this way. Follow the numbers to read from step to step.

STEP 2 A worker pours the colored wax into a **mold**. The mold has spaces shaped like crayons. The wax fills up the spaces.

STEP 3 The wax dries inside the spaces. A worker turns the mold over. Hard crayons come out!

STEP 4 The crayons go to a machine. The machine puts labels on the crayons. The labels say the color of the crayon.

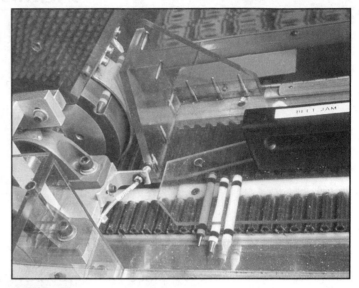

STEP 5 Different colored crayons come together on a moving belt.

STEP 6 The belt takes the crayons to boxes. The crayons go into the boxes. Finally, the crayons are ready to go to stores.

Time to color!

100 Years of Crayons for Kids

Did you know there was a time when kids did not have crayons? The first box of crayons for kids was made 100 years ago. Before that, crayons were made just for grown-up artists. Today, artists of all ages can color!

Making Crayons

Fill in the circle next to the right answer.

1. What are crayons made of?
    - (A) chalk
    - (B) wax
    - (C) wood
    - (D) metal

2. A factory is a _____ .
    - (A) place where you buy things
    - (B) school
    - (C) place where things are made
    - (D) library

3. What happens after the wax is melted?
    - (A) It is mixed with colored powder.
    - (B) A label is put on it.
    - (C) It goes into boxes.
    - (D) It goes to stores.

Write your answer.

4. What are two things that machines do in a crayon factory?

    _____

    _____

5. What are two things people do in a crayon factory?

    _____

    _____

Scholastic Teaching Resources   *Nonfiction Passages With Graphic Organizers for Independent Practice*

What's the Order?

Put the steps in order from 1 to 6. Find the sentence that tells what happens first. Write 1 on the line. Then find what happens next. Write 2 on the line. Keep going in order until you get to Step 6.

_____ The wax is melted.

_____ Labels are put on the crayons.

_____ The wax is poured into molds.

_____ Boxes of crayons go to stores.

_____ Hard crayons come out of the molds.

_____ The crayons go into boxes.

Write About It

How do you make a peanut butter and jelly sandwich? Think about what you do first, what you do next, and so on. Write the steps. Start with Step 1. Be sure you put the steps in the right order.

A Chief in the Family

Anaweg Smith, of Sapulpa, Oklahoma, is like many other 8-year-olds. She plays with her two dogs, sings in a choir, and plays soccer. But unlike most kids, Anaweg is the daughter of an Indian chief!

Chief Chad Smith, Anaweg's father, has been leader of the Cherokee Nation for three years. The job keeps him very busy. He often travels to Washington, D.C., and other places around the country.

Part of Chief Smith's job is to attend, or go to, lots of meetings. At the meetings, he talks about future plans for the Cherokee Nation. Anaweg sometimes goes to these meetings, but they're not always fun. "There's not a lot of stuff for kids there," she says.

Cherokee powwows and stomp dances are much more fun for Anaweg. At these gatherings, Chief Smith and the Cherokee celebrate their culture, or way of life. At stomp dances, for example, they sing and dance around a fire.

Anaweg says her father is busy a lot, but he does make time to drive her to soccer practice.

Men and women can be elected chief of the Cherokee Nation. But Anaweg doesn't want to follow in her father's footsteps. She's proud of him, but says, "I want to work in a zoo and help animals. As chief, you go to too many meetings, and you're away from home too much!"

Native Names

Did you know that 28 states in the U.S. got their names from American Indian words? Here are just a few:

STATE	LANGUAGE	WHAT IT MEANS
Alaska	Aleutian	"land that is not an island"
Connecticut	Mahican	"long river place"
Kansas	Sioux	"south-wind people"
Missouri	Algonquin	"river of the big canoes"
Ohio	Iroquois	"good river"
Utah	Navajo	"high up"
Wyoming	Algonquin	"large prairie place"

Fact File

- The Cherokee are currently the largest Native American tribe in the United States.
- They originally lived in North Carolina and Tennessee.
- In 1838–1839 the Cherokee were forced to leave their homes and move to a reservation in Oklahoma. Because many died, this is known as the Trail of Tears.
- The most famous Cherokee is Sequoyah. He made a writing system for spoken Cherokee.

A Chief in the Family

Fill in the circle next to the correct answer.

1. Which Native American nation does the girl in the article belong to?
   - (A) Anaweg
   - (B) Navajo
   - (C) Cherokee
   - (D) Algonquin

2. How is the girl in the article different from most other girls?
   - (A) She plays soccer.
   - (B) She has pets.
   - (C) Her dad travels for work.
   - (D) Her dad is a chief.

3. The **culture** of a group of people is their _____ .
   - (A) leader
   - (B) way of life
   - (C) special celebrations
   - (D) relatives

4. Which state's name has nothing to do with rivers?
   - (A) Ohio
   - (B) Connecticut
   - (C) Wyoming
   - (D) Missouri

5. Underline all the things that the girl in the article does, such as play soccer or go to a stomp dance. Circle those things that you also do.

Scholastic Teaching Resources   *Nonfiction Passages With Graphic Organizers for Independent Practice*

A Chief in the Family

Many states were listed in the article. Find each state. Color in the state and label it with the correct abbreviation.

STATES AND THEIR ABBREVIATIONS

AK Alaska   CT Connecticut   OH Ohio

KS Kansas   MO Missouri   UT Utah   WY Wyoming

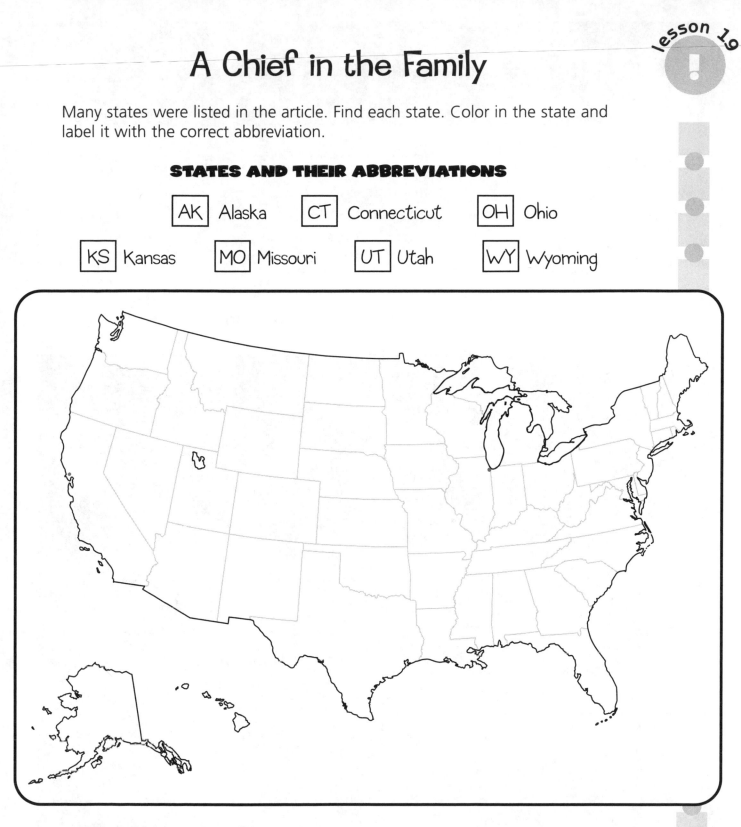

Write About It

Find out more about one of the American Indian groups in the article. Create a poster telling about this group of people. Where did they live? What were their homes like? What language did they speak? How did they dress?

DIGGING BONES

A Look at Skeletons

Dogs and kids have a lot in common. They like to eat, sleep, and play. And they're both mammals, having hair. Look at the image on this page. You'll see even more ways dogs and kids are alike, especially in what's under their fuzzy skins.

For one thing, both humans and dogs are vertebrates, animals with backbones. And of course, being land dwellers, both have lungs with protective ribs.

Look at the picture and compare these two bony skeletons. Find more details on how dogs and humans are alike and different.

BEHIND THE SCENES

What you can't see is that this amazing picture is not an X-ray, although it looks just like one. It's a computer-generated image. To create it, a team examined X-rays of dogs and humans. They even X-rayed a bicycle. Then computer artists drew three-dimensional models of each thing— even the bike helmet—on a computer. They studied how each thing moves. Finally, they created computer images of what looks like a moving X-ray!

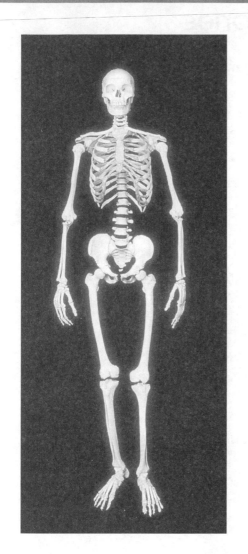

KID VS. DOG

Compare skeletons. What looks the same? What looks different?

	KID	DOG
Number of bones as an adult	206	321
Number of vertebrae	33	50
Number of joints	more than 200	more than 300
Age of maturity	18 years	2 years
Longest bone	femur (thighbone)	ulna (arm bone)
Smallest bone	ossicles (ear bones)	ossicles (ear bones)
Number of ribs	12 on each side	13 on each side

Digging Bones

Fill in the circle next to the correct answer.

1. The smallest bones in both skeletons are the _____ .
   - Ⓐ thighbones
   - Ⓑ arm bones
   - Ⓒ ear bones
   - Ⓓ ribs

2. A dog's bones are **mature**, or fully grown, _____ .
   - Ⓐ at the same age as a kid
   - Ⓑ at an earlier age than a kid
   - Ⓒ at a later age than a kid
   - Ⓓ when the dog is 5 years old

3. If skeletons did not have joints, they would _____ .
   - Ⓐ not be able to move
   - Ⓑ not grow
   - Ⓒ fall over
   - Ⓓ have more bones

4. A dog has _____ bones. A kid does not.
   - Ⓐ rib
   - Ⓑ tail
   - Ⓒ leg
   - Ⓓ neck

5. Which word means the same thing as **vertebrae**?
   - Ⓐ skeleton
   - Ⓑ x-ray
   - Ⓒ ribs
   - Ⓓ backbone

Digging Bones

Complete the graphic organizer below. List how a kid and a dog are alike and different.

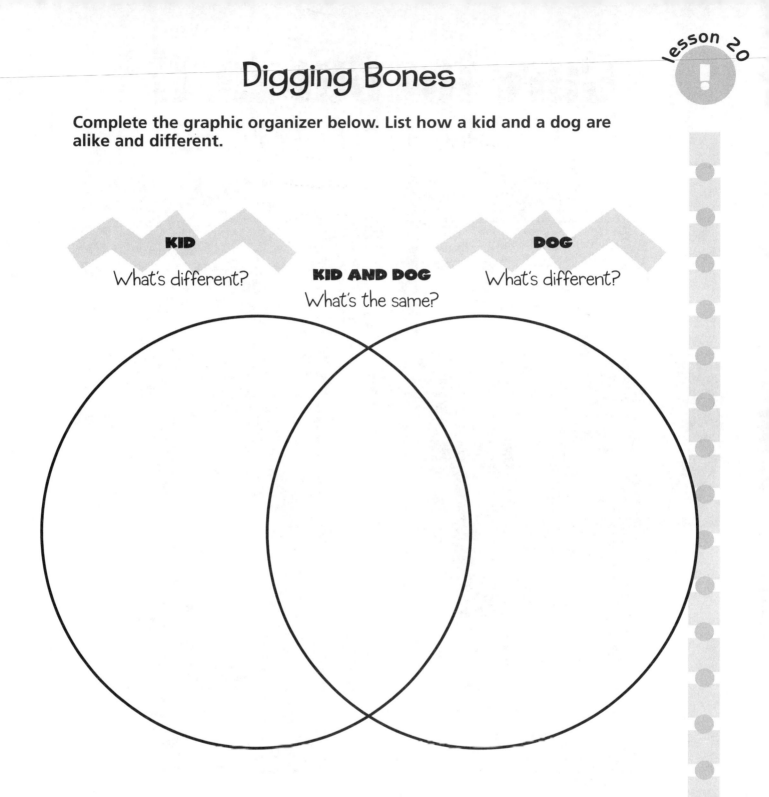

KID
What's different?

KID AND DOG
What's the same?

DOG
What's different?

Write About It

Use pipe cleaners to make a kid or dog skeleton. Glue the skeleton on paper. Then write three facts you learned about skeletons.

Nonfiction Passages With Graphic Organizers for Independent Practice

Care for Our Earth!

Earth Helpers Solve Problems!

Hi. I'm Emily. My friends and I care about our **Earth.** We love the trees, the land, and air. That's why we help our Earth when it needs help!

Earth

REMEMBER
THE THREE **R**'s
ALL YEAR LONG:

Reduce the amount of water and paper you use!

Reuse paper, boxes, jars, and bottles!

Recycle as much as possible!
And buy recycled products, too!

These kids know how to help our Earth!

paper

The recycling club at Dexter School in Fort Benning, Georgia

PROBLEM: People throw away too much **paper**. There isn't enough space on Earth to put it.

SOLUTION: Children at a school in Georgia started a recycling club. Every week, the children and their teacher recycle paper. They send it to a recycling center. It gets made into new paper.

trash

Elementary school children cleaning up the beach in Galveston, Texas

PROBLEM: People leave **trash** on this beach in Texas. Trash can get into the ocean and harm animals.

SOLUTION: These children clean the beach. They put all the trash in bags and take it away. Now it can't harm animals.

pollution

Tree Musketeers in El Segundo, California

tree

PROBLEM: The air in a California town wasn't clean enough. It was full of pollution.

SOLUTION: Children who live in the town planted trees. Trees help clean the air. The kids belong to a group called Tree Musketeers. The tiny trees they planted will grow tall.

EARTH-HELPER CHECKLIST

You can help the Earth every day! Put a ✔ next to things you already do.

Draw a 🙂 next to things you are going to do.

○ You can save water! Turn off the faucet when you brush your teeth.

○ You can save electricity! Turn off the light when you leave the room.

○ Turn off the TV when you're not watching it.

○ You can recycle trash! Bottles, cans, and newspapers can be recycled. Put these things in a recycling bin instead of in the trashcan.

Fact File

• April 22 is Earth Day.

• People around the world celebrate the good things that have been done to help our planet. But that's not all. They keep working on what still needs to be done.

Care for Our Earth!

Fill in the circle next to the correct answer.

1. A word that means the same thing as **trash** is _____ .
   - Ⓐ paper
   - Ⓑ garbage
   - Ⓒ water
   - Ⓓ trees

2. What happens to recycled paper?
   - Ⓐ It gets burned up.
   - Ⓑ It gets dumped into the ocean.
   - Ⓒ It gets saved for many years.
   - Ⓓ It is made into new paper.

3. Trash in the ocean _____ .
   - Ⓐ can harm ocean animals
   - Ⓑ can harm ships
   - Ⓒ sinks to the bottom of the sea
   - Ⓓ does not harm anything

4. When we recycle something, we _____ .
   - Ⓐ keep it
   - Ⓑ throw it into the garbage
   - Ⓒ use it again
   - Ⓓ drop it on the street

5. How do trees help us? Write your answer. Then, <u>underline</u> the sentence in the article that tells you the information.

   _____

   _____

Where Can We Help?

The people who live in this house want to help the Earth, but they're not sure how. Look at the picture. Then, follow the directions below.

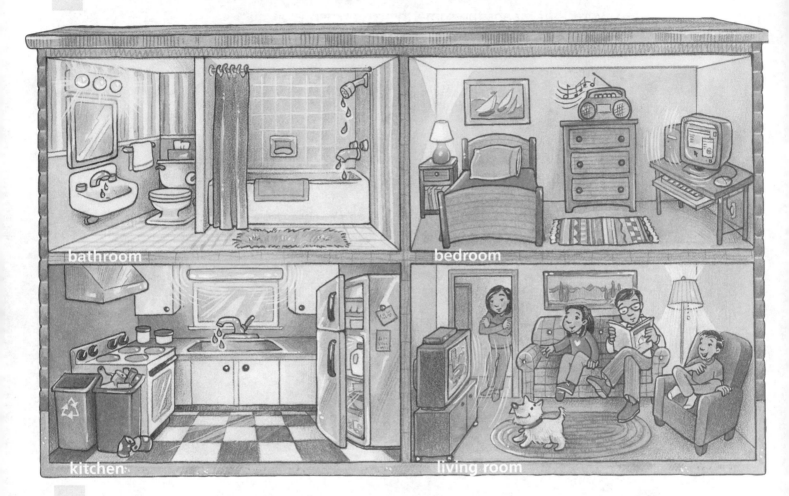

bathroom

bedroom

kitchen

living room

1. Circle the places where the people could help save water.

2. Put an ✗ on the places where the people could help save electricity.

3. Put an ✔ where the people could help recycle trash.

Write About It

Make a poster about the three R's of helping to care for our Earth.

BLAST-OFF!

It won't replace the airplane anytime soon. But the SoloTrek XFV is a machine that may one day give people a new way to zip through the sky.

The SoloTrek XFV was created by Michael Moshier. Moshier says he came up with the idea for the SoloTrek because he's "always dreamed of being able to fly." The SoloTrek is flown by a single pilot, who straps into the device and uses controls built into the handles. The machine uses fans, an engine, and built-in electronics to get it off the ground.

Experts say the SoloTrek will one day be able to fly as high as 8,000 feet. That's about eight times higher than the whole Empire State Building in New York City! Its speed will reach 80 miles per hour—a little faster than a speeding car on a highway.

WORD WISE

This guide will help you with words in the article that you may not know how to pronounce.

machine (muh-SHEEN)

millennium (muh-LEN-ee-uhm)

device (di-VISSE)

invention (in-VEN-shuhn)

electronics (i-lec-TRON-iks)

SIMPLE MACHINES

Simple machines are often small parts of larger machines. Most inventions have one or more simple machines inside them. The SoloTrek XFV has them all!

- An **inclined plane** helps you move heavy objects down from high places. A ramp on a moving van is one example.

- A **wedge** is used to push things apart, or to keep things from closing. A doorstop is one example.

- A **lever** is used to lift or open something. If you put a heavy object on one side, the other side goes up. A bottle opener is one example.

- A **screw** is used to hold two things together. Look at all the objects around you—you're bound to find screws in at least one of them!

- A **wheel and axle** spin around and help move things from place to place. You can find a wheel and axle on a wagon, a car, or an eggbeater.

- A **pulley** is a rope attached to a wheel. You pull one side of the rope to move something on the other side. A pulley can be found on a flagpole or a well.

Blast-Off!

Fill in the circle next to the correct answer.

1. Which simple machine is used to hold things together?
   - (A) wedge
   - (B) lever
   - (C) pulley
   - (D) screw

2. Another name for this article could be _____ .
   - (A) The SoloTrek XFV
   - (B) Inventing Planes and Other Flying Machines
   - (C) The Life of a Pilot
   - (D) Simple Machines

3. A **pilot** is a person who _____ .
   - (A) invents things
   - (B) flies planes
   - (C) drives fast cars
   - (D) bakes pies

4. A wheelchair ramp leading up to a building is an example of _____ .
   - (A) a wheel and axle
   - (B) a wedge
   - (C) an inclined plane
   - (D) a screw

5. Underline three sentences in the article that describe the SoloTrek XFV.

Blast-Off!

Complete the chart below.

SIMPLE MACHINE	PICTURE	EXAMPLE
inclined plane		ramp
wedge		
lever		
screw		
wheel and axle		
pulley		

Write About It

Draw a picture of you flying in the SoloTrek XFV. Write about the trip you would take in this new machine.

SEW MANY SECRETS

Slave owners tried hard to stop Harriet Tubman. They often posted rewards for her capture, but Tubman continued to **assist**, or help, hundreds of slaves without ever getting caught. How was she able to succeed? She passed information to the slaves by using special codes the slave owners couldn't understand.

These secret codes told the slaves how and where to meet Tubman for their escape. The codes were sewn into the patches of quilts. Each patch had a different **symbol**, or sign, that showed slaves important steps they needed to follow. Some of these codes are shown in the quilt patches below.

Quilt Patch

What It Meant

This patch shows stars. It told slaves to look for the North Star in the sky, and follow it north to freedom.

This pattern is called Flying Geese. The darkest arrows told slaves in what direction they should travel. Here, the darkest arrows are at the top left. This told the slaves to go west.

The Wagon Wheel is a famous symbol. It told slaves to pack their bags for their escape—just as if they were preparing for a wagon trip.

Beyond the Underground Railroad

Harriet Tubman in her later years.

Harriet Tubman made her last Underground Railroad trip in 1860, but her work with people did not stop there. During the Civil War, Tubman helped the army **liberate**, or free, slaves from the homes of slave owners.

In 1896, Tubman helped form the National Association of Colored Women. This group worked to educate people about issues that were important to African-American women.

These issues included better jobs and schooling, and women's right to vote.

Fact File

1819 or 1820	Harriet Tubman was born into slavery in Maryland.
1849	Tubman escaped to Philadelphia, Pennsylvania. There she learned how the Underground Railroad worked.
1851	She went back to Maryland to rescue her two brothers. There was a $40,000 reward for her capture, but she went back again to rescue her parents.
1860	By 1860, Tubman had led about 300 people to freedom on the Underground Railroad.
1913	Harriet Tubman died in Auburn, New York.
2003	March 10th was declared Harriet Tubman Day in New York.

Sew Many Secrets

Fill in the circle next to the correct answer.

1. Slaves needed to keep their escape plans a secret from _____ .
   - Ⓐ Harriet Tubman
   - Ⓑ other slaves
   - Ⓒ the slave owners
   - Ⓓ the quilt makers

2. The codes gave the slaves _____ .
   - Ⓐ directions for their escape
   - Ⓑ a reward
   - Ⓒ something to read
   - Ⓓ railroad tickets

3. The Wagon Wheel patch meant _____ .
   - Ⓐ you will ride in a wagon
   - Ⓑ go west
   - Ⓒ follow the North Star
   - Ⓓ pack your bags

4. Another word for **symbol** is _____ .
   - Ⓐ sign
   - Ⓑ help
   - Ⓒ free
   - Ⓓ quilt

5. <u>Underline</u> the three boldfaced words in the article. Then, ⟨circle⟩ another word in the sentence that tells what one of the boldfaced words means.

Quilt Code

Draw another quilt patch with a code that could be used to help escaping slaves. Then write what your code means.

QUILT PATCH

WHAT IT MEANS

Write About It

Find out about other secret codes that were sewn into slave quilts. Write about one of the codes. Then, draw a picture of the quilt pattern.

Dinner Time!

Slurp . . . Crunch . . . Gulp! Make way for animal digestion!

What was the last thing you ate? Chances are, it's still making its way around your body. From the first bite of food, your body kicks into digestion mode. Your mouth, esophagus, stomach, and major organs turn food into nutrients and, eventually, waste.

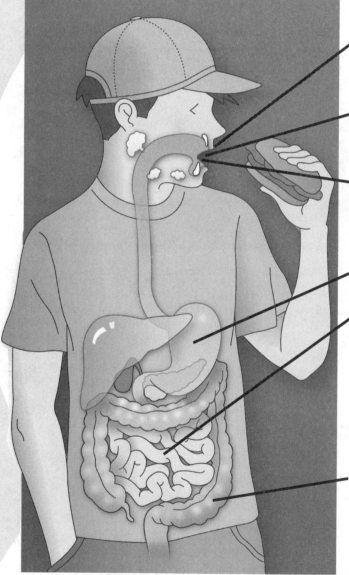

THE FOOD TRAIL

1 Digestion begins the moment food enters your **mouth**. Your teeth grind food into small pieces.

2 **Saliva** flows into your mouth as you chew. Your saliva, or spit, contains enzymes that help to break down food.

3 Your tongue forms the food into a ball and pushes it down the **esophagus**, which then squeezes the ball into your stomach.

4 In the **stomach**, acids break the ball into mush.

5 The mush flows into the **small intestine**, where it's sprayed with digestive juices from other organs, such as the pancreas, liver, and gall bladder. This breaks the food down further and allows nutrients to pass through your blood to your cells.

6 Food is then sent to the **large intestine**, where water and remaining nutrients are absorbed. Since the rest is waste that can't be used by your body, it's eventually eliminated.

Other animals digest food too, but many have a tougher job than people do. After all, we eat our food cleaned, cooked, and without any bones. Animals, however, don't have that luxury. Keep reading to find out how some wild critters open up and chow down.

Big Gulp

Imagine swallowing an entire watermelon—whole! It may be impossible for you to open your mouth that wide, but it isn't for most snakes. These slithering reptiles are experts at gulping down **prey** that's much bigger than their head.

The key to a snake's swallowing success lies in its jaws. A snake's jaws are attached to its skull by a super-stretchy ligament that allows its top and bottom jaws to detach from each other and open up to 150 degrees. How wide is that? Open your mouth as wide as you can. That's only about 45 degrees!

Once a snake captures a meal, enzymes in the saliva break down the prey's soft tissue. For tougher objects—such as hair, claws, and bones—many snakes unleash **venom**. This powerful substance not only stops prey from moving, but it helps break down any parts that are tough to eat.

After lunch, a snake heads for a snooze in the sun. The snake uses the sun's warmth to generate the heat needed to digest its meal. The heat rots the food and sends it to the intestine, which absorbs any nutrients. If the snake can't get into the sun to heat up, it may vomit the entire meal.

Liquid Lunch

Most spiders weave sticky webs to catch lunch, but some pounce and bite down with sharp teeth. Whatever their method, spiders spit power-packed **enzymes** onto their prey. The enzymes turn the prey into liquid, which the spider then sucks up.

The sucking action sends the liquid prey into the spider's stomach, where muscles shrink and expand to process the meal. The liquid is then sent to an organ called the caeca (SEE-kuh), which releases more enzymes. The caeca also stores the liquid and sends nutrients throughout the body.

Open Wide!

The black swallower fish may only be 9 inches long, but it sure packs a powerful bite. This deep-sea dweller can eat fish more than twice its own size. How? The swallower uses its massive jaws and two long upper teeth, which form an "X," to grab and hold on to its

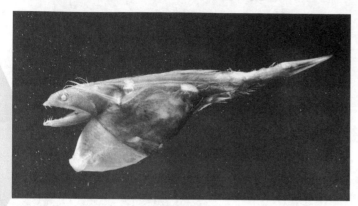

prey. The swallower's jaws then **unhinge**. This allows the fish to open its mouth wide enough to take in its massive meal.

Once the prey is gulped down, the swallower's stretchy stomach expands to make room for its supper. For an extra-large catch, the swallower creates more room by opening its rear fin. Enzymes are then released into the stomach to break down the meal—but not without consequences. As the meal is digested, the swallower's stomach fills with gas. This causes the creepy critter to float toward the surface like a helpless balloon!

Super-Sized Meal

An adult giraffe grows up to 18 feet tall and weighs over 1,700 pounds. What keeps this huge animal energized? Leaves—and lots of them. Giraffes eat up to 75 pounds of leaves a day. Now that's a tall order!

Digesting all that food is hard work. It's no wonder, then, that a giraffe is a **ruminant** (ROO-muh-nunt)—an animal whose stomach has four chambers. When a giraffe swallows, the food travels down the esophagus and into the first stomach chamber. Here it's turned into nutrients the animal can use. The remaining food is made into a ball of mush, or **cud**. The cud gets forced back up the esophagus and into the mouth. Giraffes can spend eight hours a day chewing the cud.

When giraffes finally swallow the cud, it passes through all four stomach chambers. The chambers work to remove extra fluid, and use enzymes to break the food down further. The digestion process comes to an end when the food that can't be fully digested is sent to the intestines and turned into waste.

To lick up food—like these thorny leaves— giraffes stretch their tongues up to 18 inches.

Dinner Time!

Fill in the circle next to the correct answer.

1. Which of your body organs does <u>not</u> directly help you digest food?
   - Ⓐ stomach
   - Ⓑ esophagus
   - Ⓒ heart
   - Ⓓ intestine

2. Which of the following animals is a reptile?
   - Ⓐ giraffe
   - Ⓑ snake
   - Ⓒ fish
   - Ⓓ spider

3. The word **prey** is another name for an animal's _____ .
   - Ⓐ enemy
   - Ⓑ stomach
   - Ⓒ parent
   - Ⓓ food

4. What do all the animals in the article get from food that they need to survive?
   - Ⓐ enzymes
   - Ⓑ saliva
   - Ⓒ cud
   - Ⓓ nutrients

5. Ⓒircle the name of each animal in the article. <u>Underline</u> two sentences that tell something interesting about each animal.

Dinner Time!

Complete the chart below.

ANIMAL	WHAT IT EATS	INTERESTING FACT
snake		
spider		
black swallower fish		
giraffe		

Write About It

Make a menu for your favorite dinner. Add a drawing to your menu.

What has four legs, two tusks, and 22 windows?
It's Lucy, a six-story-high elephant in Margate, New Jersey.

House with a Trunk

Each of Lucy's ears is 10 feet across and weighs one ton! Lucy's eyes are little round windows.

Reading Tip

This article describes an unusual house. The photos and captions will help you better understand what the article tells you.

- Look carefully at the photographs. They will help you picture what you are reading about.

- Be sure to read the captions. They explain what's in the photographs. They give you more information, too.

In 1881, James Lafferty, Jr. wanted to build something REALLY different and unusual in Margate. He hoped lots of visitors would come to see it and then buy homes in Margate.

So Lafferty designed a building in the shape of a giant elephant.

Builders nailed together close to a million pieces of wood to make this elephant shape. Then they covered the wood with tin, a kind of metal. The inside of the elephant had six floors and was divided into rooms. Stairs in the leg of the elephant led up into the body, which was painted pink. Last of all, a howdah (HOW-duh) was built on Lucy's back. When the elephant was finished, it weighed 90 tons!

This is a close-up of Lucy's foot.

From the howdah, visitors can see for miles around.

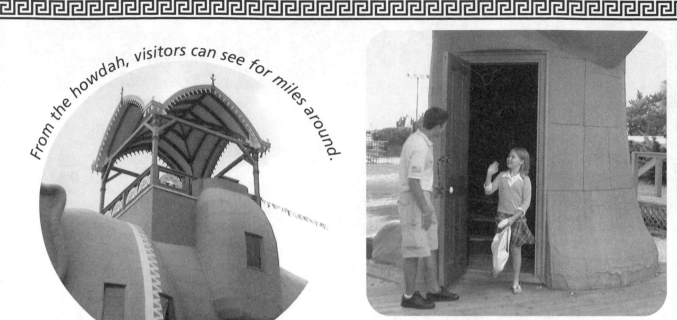

Visitors enter and exit through doors in Lucy's feet. A winding staircase goes up from the feet to the body. Altogether, there are 350 steps inside Lucy.

At one time, Lucy was a summer home. Later, Lucy was a restaurant. Today, it is a museum (myoo-ZEE-uhm) of Lucy's history.

Over the years, Lucy faced many storms and hurricanes. Luckily, the elephant did not fall down, but it was badly damaged. In 1970, The "Save Lucy Committee" raised money to fix the rundown beast. Builders made the elephant stronger. They added steel to the body and concrete to the toes. Lucy's toes have to hold up her 90-ton body.

But Lucy still had problems. The town of Margate is on the Atlantic coast, so the air is very **humid**. That means it contains many tiny droplets of water. All this water in the air began to rot the wood that Lucy was made of. Now a machine called a dehumidifier removes water from the air inside Lucy. So this beastly building should stand up for a long time!

Here is the inside of Lucy's head. The two small round windows at the end are Lucy's eyes.

House With a Trunk

Fill in the circle next to the correct answer.

1. Lucy is as tall as a _____ .
   - (A) 6-story building
   - (B) real elephant
   - (C) 22-story building
   - (D) school bus

2. **Tin** is a kind of _____ .
   - (A) wood
   - (B) elephant
   - (C) building
   - (D) metal

3. Why do you think the builders covered the wood body with metal?
   - (A) Tin looked better than wood.
   - (B) Metal lasts longer than wood.
   - (C) The metal was shiny.
   - (D) They didn't have enough wood.

4. What was the biggest danger to the building?
   - (A) airplanes
   - (B) bad weather
   - (C) too many visitors
   - (D) sun

5. From the **howdah**, people could probably see _____ .
   - (A) California
   - (B) the Pacific Ocean
   - (C) the Atlantic Ocean
   - (D) Texas

House With a Trunk

Finish the word web. Write words that tell what Lucy looks like on the outside and on the inside. Add as many lines as you need.

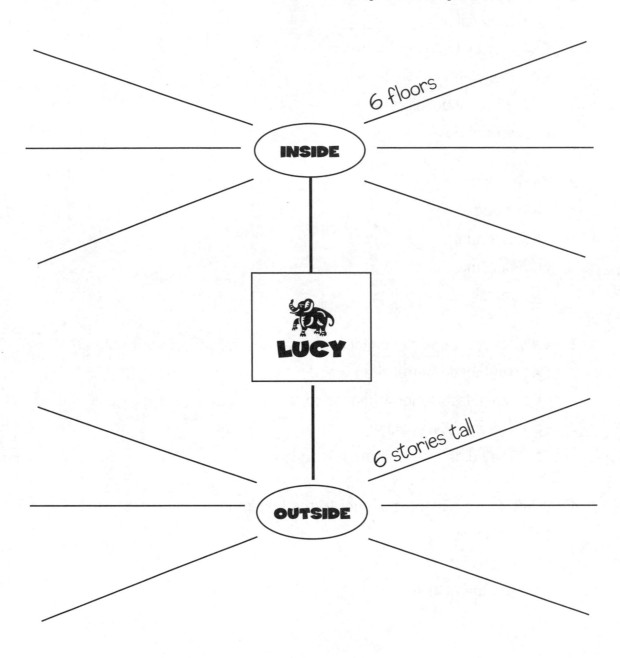

INSIDE

6 floors

LUCY

6 stories tall

OUTSIDE

Write About It ✏

Design your own building. What shape would you choose? An animal?
A fish? Draw a sketch of your building. Then write a short description of
the outside and the inside.

Every four years, we elect a new President. On Presidents' Day, we honor two past Presidents. We remember them for their leadership, honesty, and fairness.

OUR PRESIDENTIAL PAST

This painting shows Washington and his troops crossing the Delaware River to fight enemy soldiers in New Jersey.

Lincoln delivers a speech to U.S. citizens.

Leadership

During the Revolutionary War (1776–1781), George Washington led the American army against the British. The British had a much bigger army than Washington's. Washington and his troops also had to **endure**, or put up with, terrible weather and sickness. But Washington's strong and brave leadership helped America win the war. This led to his being elected our first President.

Honesty

Our 16th President, Abraham Lincoln, was known for his honesty. People even called him "Honest Abe." Honesty is an important quality for a leader to have. People want to feel that they can trust their leaders. People want to believe what their leaders tell them.

Fairness

One of the most important things President Lincoln did was end slavery in America. This brought freedom to all the African Americans who lived as slaves. Lincoln believed that all people should be treated as equals, even though many people at that time did not share his opinion.

Fact File

- In the 1700s, America belonged to England. The people here had to obey the laws made by England. They did not think the laws were fair.

- Americans went to war with England. They were fighting to have their own country and make their own laws.

- George Washington was a general in the American army.

- England was also called Britain. So, the English people were called the British.

Our Presidential Past

Fill in the circle next to the correct answer.

1. Before he was President, George Washington was a _____ .
   - (A) boat builder
   - (B) soldier
   - (C) doctor
   - (D) writer

2. George Washington was elected President because _____ .
   - (A) no one else wanted to be President
   - (B) people knew he was a good leader
   - (C) he owned a lot of land
   - (D) he made good speeches

3. What does the word **endure** mean?
   - (A) get sick from cold weather
   - (B) fight in a war
   - (C) put up with things that are hard to deal with
   - (D) go inside to keep warm and dry

4. Abraham Lincoln was honest, so people _____ .
   - (A) trusted him
   - (B) were afraid of him
   - (C) did not agree with him
   - (D) liked him

5. What is the main idea of the article?
   - (A) We elect a new President every four years.
   - (B) Presidents' Day is a holiday that we celebrate in February.
   - (C) We remember Washington and Lincoln for their leadership, honesty, and fairness.
   - (D) Abraham Lincoln was known as "Honest Abe."

Scholastic Teaching Resources   *Nonfiction Passages With Graphic Organizers for Independent Practice*

Presidential Fact File

Under each name, write at least 3 facts that the article tells you about George Washington and Abraham Lincoln.

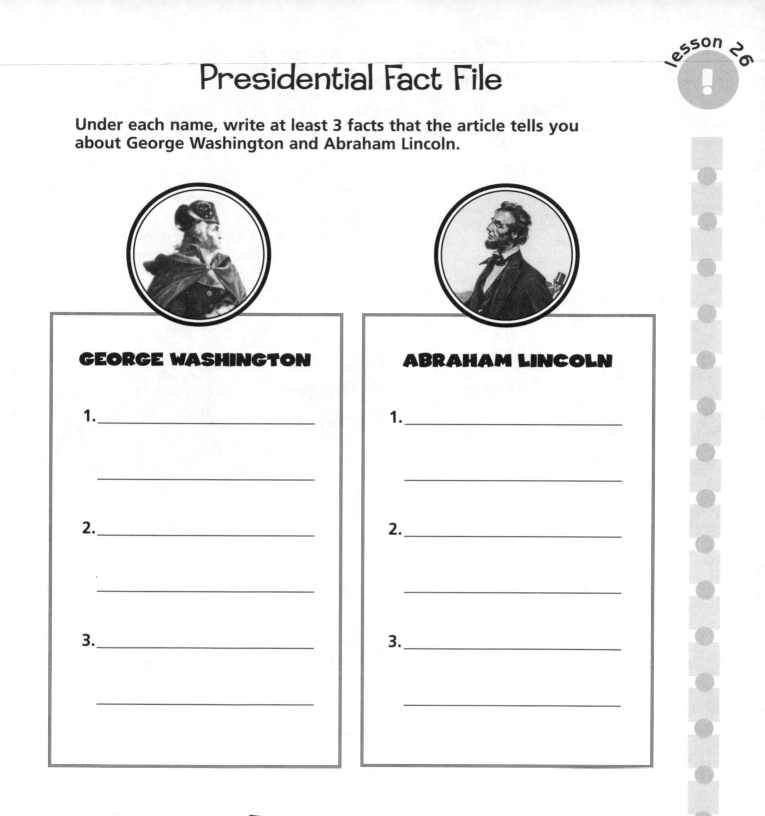

GEORGE WASHINGTON

1._____

_____

2._____

_____

3._____

_____

ABRAHAM LINCOLN

1._____

_____

2._____

_____

3._____

_____

Write About It ✏️

Think of someone else who is a good leader, an honest person, or a fair person. It might be someone you know or someone you have read about. Write what that person did that showed good leadership, honesty, or fairness.

Critters Cry for Help

Some critters may seem creepy, but they actually help keep the Earth's animal population in balance. Many of these creatures are endangered. There are not many left. Science is trying to save them before they disappear completely.

Reading Tip

All the creatures in *Critters Cry for Help* are endangered. Why? As you read the facts about each one, be sure you understand the cause, or the reason, it's endangered.

Indian Python

This snake can grow up to 25 feet long. Its body is grayish-brown, with spots of red, cream, and gold.

WHERE FOUND: In Pakistan, Nepal, and India in hot, humid forests along rivers and swamps.

DIET: It eats mice and other rodents, insects, birds, and rabbits. Some of these creatures carry diseases, which are a threat to people's health.

UNUSUAL FACTS: The Indian Python is the second-largest snake in Asia. The python wraps its body tightly around its prey and squeezes it so that it cannot breathe. The python is able to swallow its meal whole. If its prey is large, it may not eat again for a year.

SURVIVAL STATUS: Endangered because it is hunted for its skin, which is made into boots, handbags, and belts.

Mexican Red-Knee Tarantula

This fuzzy black spider has red knees. It measures $6\frac{1}{2}$ to 8 inches diagonally, from the tip of a front leg to the tip of a back leg.

WHERE FOUND: In the rain forests of Mexico.

DIET: It eats insects, small frogs, and sometimes mice.

UNUSUAL FACTS: This spider is usually peaceful. However, when it is threatened, it rears up and shows the red bristles on its body. Its home is a burrow in the ground, which the spider lines with spider silk. The Mexican red-knee tarantula has eight eyes around its head, so it can see both forward and backward. Scientists think the venom of this poisonous spider may hold hope as a treatment for certain diseases.

SURVIVAL STATUS: Endangered because its habitat is being destroyed. Also, people capture the spiders to sell as pets.

Sonoran Green Toad

Australian Ghost Bat

This gray-skinned bat measures 2 feet from wing tip to wing tip and 4 to 5 $\frac{1}{2}$ inches from head to foot. It also has enormous 2-inch ears.

WHERE FOUND: Hot and humid areas of Australia.

DIET: This bat is one of the few carnivorous, or meat-eating, bats. It eats snakes, insects, frogs, and birds.

UNUSUAL FACTS: The ghost bat gets its name from the fact that it is light gray, almost white. The bat makes a cricket-like chirping sound.

SURVIVAL STATUS: Endangered because the mines and caves where the bats live are being destroyed.

This black, green, and yellow toad is only 2 inches long from nose to tail.

WHERE FOUND: In southern Arizona and parts of Mexico.

UNUSUAL FACTS: The male makes a buzzing sound to attract the female. The toad's skin is covered with small bumps.

SURVIVAL STATUS: Endangered because its home is being wiped out.

ANIMALS IN DANGER

This chart shows how many other animals are endangered (in danger of dying out) or threatened (likely to become endangered).

Group of Animals	Number of Endangered Species	Number of Threatened Species
Mammals	55	9
Birds	74	16
Reptiles	14	19
Amphibians	7	6
Fish	65	40
Insects	20	9

Critters Cry for Help

Fill in the circle next to the correct answer.

1. The ghost bat, tarantula, and green toad are endangered because _____ .
   - (A) people are afraid of them
   - (B) people are destroying where they live
   - (C) people hunt them for their skins
   - (D) people hunt them for food

2. The Sonoran Green Toad is _____ .
   - (A) a reptile
   - (B) a fish
   - (C) an insect
   - (D) an amphibian

3. Which group of animals has the most endangered species?
   - (A) birds
   - (B) mammals
   - (C) fish
   - (D) reptiles

4. The word **venom** means _____ .
   - (A) spider
   - (B) disease
   - (C) poison
   - (D) rodents, such as rats and mice

5. Look at the chart in the article.
   - • Circle the group of animals that has the most endangered species.
   - • Put an ✘ on the number that shows how many species of fish are endangered.
   - • Put a ✔ on the number that shows the species that is most threatened.

What's the Cause?

Tell the cause, or why, the creatures below are endangered.

Indian Python

Cause? _____

_____

_____

_____

_____

_____

_____

Mexican Red-Knee Tarantula

Cause? _____

_____

_____

_____

_____

_____

EFFECT
All are endangered.

Sonoran Green Toad

Cause? _____

_____

_____

_____

_____

_____

_____

Australian Ghost Bat

Cause? _____

_____

_____

_____

_____

_____

_____

Write About It ✏️

The swift fox, river otter, bald eagle, and alligator were once endangered. Today they are no longer on the list of endangered animals. Do some research to find out how one of these animals was saved.

COULD YOUR BODY GO TO MARS?

Space travel might change you in surprising ways.

Reading Tip

The article you are about to read explains the **causes** and **effects** on your body of traveling to Mars.

As you read,

- identify the causes, or what happens.

- find out why these things happen, or the effects.

- look for key words and phrases such as *because*, *then*, *so*, and *as a result*.

On October 24, 2001, the unpiloted *Mars Odyssey* spacecraft began orbiting, or circling, the red planet. Could human visitors be next? Scientists at NASA are studying what would happen to the human body during such a long space trip. Read on, then decide: Would you like to go to Mars?

NO FUN AT LUNCH Fluid-filled canals in your inner ear help your brain know rightside–up from upside–down. But leave Earth's atmosphere, and you leave the planet's gravity behind. Without its strong pull, your balance will be off. For the first few days, you'll have a bad case of motion sickness.

BRITTLE BONES Your bones make up your skeletal system—the frame that holds your body together. On Earth, the pressure of your body weight causes your bones to grow thick and strong. Without this pressure, bones become fragile. That means they could break easily.

THE SKINNY IN SPACE In the zero gravity of space, objects—including your body—are nearly weightless. So your muscles don't get much of a workout. Unused muscles shrink. After weeks in space, your big thigh muscles would look like a peeled apple left out to dry.

WEAK BEATER Your heart, too, will shrink in space. As the heart beats slower, it pumps less oxygen to your brain and other organs. That means you will feel very tired.

QUICK FIX With exercise, your body can fight some of these changes. For example, special treadmills and weight machines have helped astronauts keep strong muscles. But even with fancy equipment, the journey to Mars will be difficult—the solar system's toughest road trip.

Could Your Body Go to Mars?

Fill in the circle next to the correct answer.

1. Which of the following is <u>not</u> true?

   Ⓐ It would take over two years to travel to Mars.

   Ⓑ There is no gravity on Mars, so you would float in the air.

   Ⓒ NASA scientists sent two pilots to Mars on October 24, 2001.

   Ⓓ Exercise can help you stay healthy when you're in space.

2. How is your body different in space than on Earth?

   Ⓐ You body weighs more in space.

   Ⓑ Your chest and head get bigger in space.

   Ⓒ Your bones grow stronger in space.

   Ⓓ Your skin becomes more tan in space.

3. To **shrink** means to _____ .

   Ⓐ go around

   Ⓑ swell

   Ⓒ break easily

   Ⓓ get smaller

4. What would be another title for this article?

   Ⓐ Recent Travelers to Mars

   Ⓑ Your Body in Space

   Ⓒ NASA Explores the Solar System

   Ⓓ Losing Weight in Space

5. Circle three sentences in the article that describe what would happen to your body if you went to Mars.

Could Your Body Go to Mars?

Draw a picture of yourself on Earth and on Mars. Write 2 or 3 sentences that tell how your body would be different on Mars.

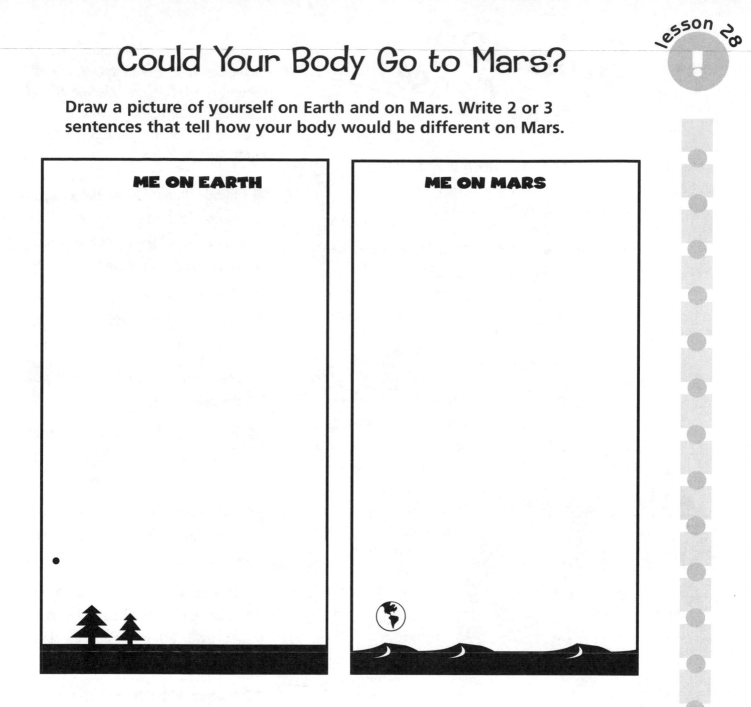

ME ON EARTH

ME ON MARS

How I would be different on Mars _____

_____

_____

Write About It

Learn more about Mars. Find 5 interesting facts about the close planet. List them on a Mars Fact Card. Add a picture to your fact card.

Spinning for a Good Cause

Figure-skater Lucinda Ruh (ROO) is renowned for her super spinning skills on ice. Now the Swiss skating champ hopes to whirl her way into the record books—and she did it for kids!

At an ice rink in New York City, Ruh aims to set two world records. One of the records is for the most spins per second. The other one is for the most spins on one foot without stopping—the record to beat is 60 spins without stopping.

Ruh is kicking off the start of her organization for helping kids—the Lucinda Ruh Share a Book Foundation. The

group will send books to kids in homeless shelters, day-care centers, and hospitals around the United States. School kids have collected books to send.

"I remember waiting in the dressing room before competitions, and to have a book with me was incredible," she says. "You can go on somebody else's journey in a book—it takes your troubles away for a while."

While Lucinda Ruh's spinning was an incredible sports feat, sportswriters around the U.S. have selected the 10 hardest things to do in sports. Number one is the hardest. Do you agree with this list?

1 Hitting a Baseball in the Major Leagues Imagine watching a ball traveling 95 miles per hour toward you, and then hitting it at just the right spot!

2 Race-Car Driving Racers must steer while driving at speeds of more than 200 miles per hour.

3 Pole Vaulting Pole vaulters need great strength and agility.

4 Hitting a Golf Ball Long and Straight Even pros struggle to hit golf balls far and accurately at the same time.

5 Returning a 130-mile-per-hour Tennis Serve Players get half a second to see and hit the ball back—inside the lines.

6 Landing a Quadruple Toe-Loop Jump After spinning four times in the air, skaters land on a 1/4-inch-wide skate blade —on ice!

7 Running a Marathon Marathon runners run 26.2 miles at a time.

8 Riding in the Tour de France Bike Race Racers ride more than 2,500 miles, often up steep mountains.

9 Saving a Penalty Kick Goalies block soccer balls flying at 60 miles per hour.

10 Downhill Ski Racing Downhill racers ski 80 miles per hour down snow-covered mountains.

Spinning for a Good Cause

Fill in the circle next to the correct answer.

1. What can Lucinda Ruh do better than anyone else?
   - (A) pole vault over ten feet high
   - (B) land a quadruple toe-loop jump on ice
   - (C) ride in the Tour de France bike race
   - (D) spin on ice skates

2. Which of the following is the most difficult?
   - (A) running in a marathon
   - (B) saving a soccer penalty kick
   - (C) driving a race car
   - (D) pole vaulting

3. The word **renowned** means the same as _____ .
   - (A) fast
   - (B) athletic
   - (C) famous
   - (D) helpful

4. Which athlete is not shown on the TOP 10 list?
   - (A) race car driver
   - (B) figure skater
   - (C) skier
   - (D) gymnast

5. Circle the sports feat in the article that is the most interesting to you. Tell why you like this sport.

   _____

   _____

Spinning for a Good Cause

Take a poll of your classmates. Record the number of students who like to play or watch each sport listed.

SPORT	NUMBER OF STUDENTS
baseball	
race-car racing	
pole vaulting	
golf	
tennis	
ice skating	
running	
bike racing	
soccer	
skiing	

Write About It

Pick a favorite sport or game. Write the rules to play that sport or game.

Celebrating 100 Years

of the

World Series

To baseball fans there is no sweeter sound than the crack of a bat hitting a baseball. Watching players hit, catch, and slide is especially exciting during October. This is when the best teams in baseball compete in the World Series.

The 2003 World Series was extra special. The 2003 baseball championship marked the 100th anniversary of the first World Series. In 1903, the Pittsburgh Pirates and the Boston Pilgrims (now the Red Sox) faced each other in eight games.

Baseball legends such as Pittsburgh shortstop Honus Wagner and Boston pitcher Cy Young played in that first series. Boston won the series by five games to three, thanks to the pitching of Cy Young and Bill Dinneen.

That first World Series anniversary was celebrated during a regular season game in 2003, when Pittsburgh and Boston played each other for the first time since 1903. For "Turn Back the Clock Night," Pittsburgh's PNC Park was made to look like it did in 1903. Players wore the same kind of uniforms as players wore 100 years ago.

A GAME OF MEMORIES

In the 1903 World Series, the first team to win five out of nine games became the world champions. In 1905, the rules were changed. Teams only had to win four out of seven games to be World Series champions. This change became permanent in 1922.

1903—The first World Series was played in Pittsburgh and at the Huntington Avenue Grounds in Boston (shown here).

The World Series has only been skipped twice. In 1904, the National League's New York Giants refused to play Boston, the American League champion. The president of the Giants thought that the American League was inferior and refused to compete. The series resumed in 1905. In 1994, a salary dispute between players and team owners caused the series to be canceled.

The American League's New York Yankees, who have played in more World Series than any other team, have won 26 times, but not in 2003.

Every World Series has great moments. There was New York Yankee's Babe Ruth hitting three home runs in Game 4 of the 1928 World Series. In 1954, Willie Mays of the New York Giants made an amazing catch on a dead run toward the centerfield wall. And in 2001, the Yankee's Derek Jeter hit a game-winning home run in the 10ᵗʰ inning of Game 4.

Each great catch, dropped ball, and ninth-inning homer becomes part of baseball history. Watch to see which team will be this year's world champs. You might even see history in the making!

Baseball Past and Present

When the first World Series was played 100 years ago, the rules of the game were about the same, but life was very different. For example, in 1903, there were no radios or TVs, so people could only see and hear a baseball game by going to the ballpark. Since the country was just starting to get electricity, games took place only during daylight hours.

WORLD SERIES	1903 Pittsburgh Pirates vs. Boston Pilgrims	2003 Florida Marlins vs. New York Yankees
World Series Ticket Prices	From 50 cents to a dollar	From $225 to $1,100
Fans	In 1903, about 11,600 attended each of the eight World Series games.	This year, about 47,000 went to each of the games, and millions more watched the series on TV.
Salary	In 1903, the average baseball player earned $2,500 a year.	Today, the average baseball player salary is about $1.1 million.
Drinks at Games	Sarsaparilla	Cola

Celebrating 100 Years
of the World Series

Fill in the circle next to the correct answer.

1. Which team won the first World Series?
   - (A) Boston Red Sox
   - (B) New York Giants
   - (C) Pittsburgh Pirates
   - (D) Boston Pilgrims

2. What did the World Series in the early 1900s have in common with the World Series today?
   - (A) ticket prices
   - (B) baseball player salaries
   - (C) game rules
   - (D) people in attendance

3. Which sentence uses the word **bat** correctly?
   - (A) The bat flew into the dark cave.
   - (B) The player hit the ball with the wooden bat.
   - (C) The cat bat the toy around.
   - (D) All of the above

4. Which game is most similar to the World Series?
   - (A) a high school basketball state championship game
   - (B) professional football's Super Bowl game
   - (C) a city's softball league game
   - (D) the Olympic track and field events

5. Underline three sentences in the article that tell about the 2003 World Series. Circle three sentences that tell about the 1903 World Series.

Celebrating 100 Years of the World Series

Fill in the World Series tickets. Use facts from the article.

World Series 1903

Where Played?

_____

Who Played?

_____

vs.

_____

Who Won?

_____

Ticket Price _____

Number of People at the Game

_____

World Series 2003

Where Played?

_____

Who Played?

_____

vs.

_____

Who Won?

_____

Ticket Price _____

Number of People at the Game

_____

Write About It ✏️

Find out more about one of the baseball players in the article. Create a baseball card for him. List facts about where he was born, where he plays, and any records he has set.

Answer Key

Go, Animals!
page 11
1. b
2. a
3. a
4. d
5. a

From Grapevine to Jelly Jar
page 15
1. d
2. c
3. c
4. d
5. Answers will vary.

Creature Feature
page 19
1. b
2. d
3. c
4. b
5. Answers will vary.

Bat at Night
page 23
1. c
2. b
3. b
4. a
5. The bat finds fruit to eat. The bat also sips nectar, the sweet juice of flowers. fruit; nectar

One Language, Many Nations
page 27
1. d
2. c
3. b
4. c
5. Answers will vary.

Seeds on the Go!
page 31
1. d
2. a
3. d
4. a
5. c

8 Reasons to Love an Octopus
Page 35
1. d
2. d
3. c
4. b
5. Answers will vary.

Pilgrim Children
page 39
1. a
2. c

3. d
4. d
5. jacket, pants, skirt, socks

How Spiders Use Silk
page 43
1. c
2. a
3. a
4. b
5. Students should circle black-and-yellow argiope, trapdoor spider, jumping spider, black widow.

Hot Spot
page 47
1. c
2. b
3. d
4. a
5. Answers will vary.

Animal Survival
page 51
1. b
2. a
3. d
4. b
5. Answers will vary.

Tooth Truth
page 54
1. d
2. c
3. d
4. c
5. Answers will vary.

Penguins of the World
page 59
1. c
2. d
3. a
4. c
5. Chinstrap; Chinstraps have a black line on their chin. Little Blue; Little blues have a blue back; These are the smallest penguins of all.

Stamp of Excellence
page 62
1. c
2. d
3. b
4. d
5. Answers will vary.

Zoos Help Out!
page 66
1. c
2. d
3. d
4. c
5. Answers will vary.

Chinese New Year
page 70
1. c
2. a
3. d
4. a
5. Answer should reflect current year;
2010; rabbit

Horsing Around
page 74
1. c
2. b
3. d
4. c
5. Answers will vary.

Making Crayons
page 78
1. b
2. c
3. a
4. Possible answers: Melt the wax, mix
the wax and colored powder, put labels
on crayons, put crayons in boxes.
5. Possible answers: Pour the colored
wax into a mold, take the crayons out
of the mold. Accept other reasonable
answers, such as: Check the machines,
check the crayons.

A Chief in the Family
page 82
1. c
2. d
3. b
4. c
5. Answers will vary.

Digging Bones
page 86
1. c
2. b
3. a
4. b
5. d

Care for Our Earth!
page 91
1. b
2. d
3. a
4. c
5. Answers will vary.

Blast-Off!
page 94
1. d
2. a
3. b
4. c
5. Answers will vary.

Sew Many Secrets
page 98
1. c
2. a
3. d
4. a
5. assist, symbol, liberate; help, sign,
or free

Dinner Time!
page 103
1. c
2. b
3. d
4. d
5. Answers will vary.

House With a Trunk
page 107
1. a
2. d
3. b
4. b
5. c

Our Presidential Past
page 110
1. b
2. b
3. c
4. a
5. c

Critters Cry for Help
page 114
1. b
2. d
3. a
4. c
5. circle around Birds; ✗ on 65; ✔ on 40

Could Your Body Go to Mars?
page 118
1. c
2. b
3. d
4. b
5. Answers will vary.

Spinning for a Good Cause
page 121
1. d
2. c
3. c
4. d
5. Answers will vary.

Celebrating 100 Years of the World Series
page 125
1. d
2. c
3. d
4. b
5. Answers will vary.